T0001172

TEN LIVES, TEN DEMANDS

TEN LIVES, TEN DEMANDS

LIFE-AND-DEATH STORIES, AND A BLACK ACTIVIST'S BLUEPRINT FOR RACIAL JUSTICE

BY SOLOMON JONES

Beacon Press
Boston

Beacon Press
Boston, Massachusetts
www.beacon.org

Beacon Press books
are published under the auspices of
the Unitarian Universalist Association of Congregations.

Printed in the United States of America

24 23 22 21 8 7 6 5 4 3 2 1

This book is printed on acid-free paper that meets the uncoated paper ANSI/NISO specifications for permanence as revised in 1992.

Text design by Nancy Koerner at Wilsted & Taylor Publishing Services

Library of Congress Cataloging-in-Publication Data

Names: Jones, Solomon, author.
Title: Ten lives, ten demands : life-and-death stories, and a black activist's blueprint for racial justice / by Solomon Jones.
Description: Boston : Beacon Press, [2021] | Includes bibliographical references.
Identifiers: LCCN 2021024306 (print) | LCCN 2021024307 (ebook) | ISBN 9780807020173 (hardcover) | ISBN 9780807020203 (ebook)
Subjects: LCSH: Racism—United States. | Racial justice—United States. | Police brutality—United States.
Classification: LCC HT1521 .J66 2021 (print) | LCC HT1521 (ebook) | DDC 305.800973—dc23
LC record available at https://lccn.loc.gov/2021024306
LC ebook record available at https://lccn.loc.gov/2021024307

To the families whose loved ones were wrongly killed by a criminal justice system that should have protected them.

CONTENTS

PREFACE
Black in the System . . . ix

1
GEORGE FLOYD
WHY WE DEMAND REPARATIONS
1

2
MICHAEL BROWN
THE CASE FOR CONSENT DECREES
11

3
HASSAN BENNETT
THE CASE FOR COMPENSATION
27

4
BREONNA TAYLOR
THE CASE FOR BODY CAMERAS
39

5
ERIC GARNER
THE CASE FOR PUBLIC RECORDS
55

6
ALTON STERLING
THE CASE FOR CHANGING FEDERAL LAW
71

7
TAMIR RICE
THE CASE FOR INDEPENDENT PROSECUTORS
85

8
TRAYVON MARTIN
THE CASE AGAINST STAND-YOUR-GROUND LAWS
103

9
DEBORAH DANNER
THE CASE FOR DEFUNDING THE POLICE
119

10
SANDRA BLAND
THE CASE FOR ENDING RACIAL PROFILING
135

EPILOGUE
151

Acknowledgments . . . 153

Notes . . . 155

PREFACE

BLACK IN THE SYSTEM

With dull and vacant eyes, I stared into the camera. My skin, normally the rich brown color of dark chocolate, was dry and gray. My unkempt hair was dirty and tightly curled. My facial expression was that of a man resigned to the belief that he would die homeless and crack addicted.

It was that picture—a mugshot from one of my seven arrests for charges ranging from retail theft to attempted burglary—that marked my first television appearance. No one was asking my opinion on CNN back then. I was simply a piper, a crackhead, a disposable cog in the wheel of a drug culture that thrived on the desperation of people like me. But on that day, when they flashed my mugshot on Philadelphia's Fox 29, I achieved an infamy normally reserved for murderers. I was one of the city's most wanted, and most viewers who saw my picture likely believed I deserved to be punished. More than two decades later, they'd believe the same thing about a Black man named George Floyd.

The narrative of Black criminality came straight from the War on Drugs, a political strategy that targeted African Americans as far back as the early 1970s. The demonization of Black addicts like myself made for entertaining television. More importantly, it served as the pretext for an all-out attack on Black communities.

That's the way John Ehrlichman, an advisor to President Richard Nixon, laid it out in a 1994 *Harper's* magazine interview, when Ehrlichman explained that Nixon's War on Drugs had two enemies: the anti-war left and Black people.

"We knew we couldn't make it illegal to be either against the war or Black, but by getting the public to associate the hippies with marijuana and Blacks with heroin and then criminalizing both heavily, we could disrupt those communities," Ehrlichman told the reporter. "We could arrest their leaders, raid their homes, break up their meetings, and vilify them night after night on the evening news."

That's exactly what happened.

On June 17, 1971, President Richard Nixon walked into a White House press briefing and said: "America's public enemy number one in the United States is drug abuse. In order to fight and defeat this enemy, it is necessary to wage a new, all-out offensive."[1]

Nixon was using the language of military conflict to describe his plan to fight drugs, and that was no accident. America's losses in Vietnam were producing ever more damaging headlines, including the 1968 murder conviction of Lieutenant William Calley, commander of the American soldiers who brutally slaughtered twenty-two Vietnamese civilians, in what became known as the My Lai Massacre. If Nixon wanted to be reelected in 1972, he desperately needed a war he could win. By announcing that the War on Drugs would be coordinated in the White House, he set himself up as the conquering hero. Hippies and Blacks would be the casualties.

Nixon not only won reelection with that strategy. He set the stage for the establishment of the Drug Enforcement Agency, and the War on Drugs became a mainstay of American politics. Even after Nixon resigned and the Vietnam War ended, thus eliminating the anti-war left, Blacks were still targeted with devastating consequences.

In 1982, as crack cocaine began to alter America's drug landscape, President Ronald Reagan said, "Drugs are bad, and we're going after them. . . . And we're going to win the war on drugs."[2]

His wife, Nancy, became the face of the infamous "Just Say No" campaign while Reagan and his political allies instituted racist laws such as the Anti-Drug Abuse Act of 1986. Under that law, distributing just five grams of crack—a low-cost form of cocaine more accessible in Black communities—carried a minimum five-year federal prison sentence. One would have to distribute 500 grams of powder cocaine—an expensive form of the drug used in affluent white communities—in order to get the same five-year federal sentence.

The drug war escalated under President George H. W. Bush, who used the DEA to lure an eighteen-year-old Black high school student named Keith Jackson to an area near the White House. Once there, Jackson sold drugs to undercover agents and was arrested in a publicity stunt that enabled Bush to brandish a bag of crack during a nationally televised speech.

Bush said at the time that solving America's drug problem would require "more prisons, more jails, more courts, more prosecutors."[3]

Over the course of his presidency, Bush made that approach a reality. He increased the federal drug control budget from $5 billion to over $12 billion, and increased the federal prison population by over sixteen thousand people in just four years. Jackson, the eighteen-year-old who sold the crack Bush showed on national television, was among the imprisoned. Though federal prosecutors did not win a conviction for the crack sale near the White House, Jackson was eventually sentenced to ten years for a previous sale to undercover agents.

That kind of sentencing became the legacy of the drug war in Black communities, where African Americans were already being disproportionately arrested and jailed for marijuana. With the advent of crack—a quick, intense, and cheap high that put men in graves and women on the streets—Black communities were in tatters. The family structure disintegrated. Drug dealing was rampant. Property crimes were common. Murder rates skyrocketed.

Black leaders asked for more police to stem the tide of drug-related violence and got much more than they bargained for. President Joe Biden, then a fourth-term US senator from Delaware and chair of the Senate Judiciary Committee, helped to write the Violent Crime Control and Law Enforcement Act of 1994. In the run-up to the bill's passage, Biden took to the Senate floor and used language that was rife with racial undertones to win his colleagues' support.

"We have predators on our streets that society has in fact, in part because of its neglect, created," Biden said during an impassioned speech. He went on to describe a "cadre of young people, tens of thousands of them, born out of wedlock, without parents, without supervision, without any structure, without any conscience developing because they literally . . . because they literally have not been socialized, they literally have not had an opportunity." Biden added that he wasn't concerned about "why someone is a malefactor in society" and that criminals needed to be kept "away from my mother, your husband, our families."[4]

At a time when political survival meant embracing a tough-on-crime stance, Biden and his white colleagues on both sides of the aisle were eager to push the legislation through. They were joined by members of the Congressional Black Caucus like long-time South Carolina Congressman

Jim Clyburn, who supported the legislation despite the racial rhetoric that made the bill palatable for conservatives.

Then president Bill Clinton, long seen as too liberal by those on the political right, enhanced his own crime-fighting bona fides by signing into law a bill known as the Violent Crime Control and Law Enforcement Act of 1994. Among other things, the legislation put tens of thousands more police officers on the streets, implemented drug courts, and gave mandatory life sentences to criminals convicted of a violent felony after two prior convictions, the infamous "three strikes" rule.

Despite the tough penalties it contained, the law didn't serve as a deterrent. The potent mix of crack cocaine and poverty drew desperate people to the drug trade and hopeless people to addiction. Instead of providing sorely needed resources, the 1994 law would ultimately accelerate mass incarceration and devastate Black communities.

For African Americans, that was a familiar outcome. Since 1619, when our ancestors were kidnapped and brought to the Americas in shackles, the dehumanization of Blacks has often taken place under the guise of upholding the law.

As Ta-Nehisi Coates notes in "The Case for Reparations," his seminal work in *The Atlantic*,

> American law worked to reduce black people to a class of untouchables and raise all white men to the level of citizens. In 1650, Virginia mandated that "all persons except Negroes" were to carry arms. In 1664, Maryland mandated that any Englishwoman who married a slave must live as a slave of her husband's master. In 1705, the Virginia assembly passed a law allowing for the dismemberment of unruly slaves—but forbidding masters from whipping "a Christian white servant naked, without an order from a justice of the peace." In that same law, the colony mandated that "all horses, cattle, and hogs, now belonging, or that hereafter shall belong to any slave" be seized and sold off by the local church, the profits used to support "the poor of the said parish."[5]

In essence, the theft of Black freedom, Black property, and Black lives was etched into the very foundations of America, and for centuries after its founding, America adopted legislation that continued to undergird the notion of white supremacy.

After American laws allowed Blacks to be stripped of property, herded into ghettoes, and denied the protection of government agents like police, the carnage that accompanied crack cocaine brought utter destruction to the Black community.

Measuring Crack Cocaine and Its Impact, a 2006 study by Harvard's Roland G. Fryer Jr. and researchers from the University of Chicago, found that in the decade between 1984 and 1994, "the homicide rate for Black males aged 14–17 more than doubled and homicide rates for Black males aged 18–24 increased almost as much."[6]

The study also found that in the Black community, fetal death rates, low birth weight babies, weapons arrests, and the number of children in foster care increased sharply during the crack era.

It was against this backdrop that the media began to exploit Black misery for America's viewing pleasure. National shows like the CBS News Special, "48 Hours on Crack Street," put a microscope on individuals who'd lost themselves in swirling clouds of smoke. In doing so, the media helped to bring about Nixon's vision of the War on Drugs, a vision that John Ehrlichman said would allow Blacks and other enemies to be vilified night after night on the evening news.

That was where I found myself on the night the local Fox affiliate displayed my mugshot and called me one of Philly's most wanted. I was the one being vilified.

I suppose the system needed another Black drug addict behind bars, or perhaps the media needed another Black story to exploit. Either way, as I stood behind a marble desk, oblivious to the fact that my mugshot was being broadcast on local television, a blond news anchor ran through my aliases and my list of petty offenses. Then he said my real name: Solomon Jones.

With that, the wreckage of my past was laid bare for all to see. The addiction. The crimes. The bench warrants. The truth. All of it confronted me in a single newscast, and the racist strategy that had survived from Nixon to Bill Clinton was on me like a heavyweight. I was now the face of America's racist War on Drugs. At least that's how I was portrayed.

In truth, I was simply a doorman. A concierge, of sorts. To the white, well-heeled residents of the condominium complex where I was employed, I was just a young man working his way through Temple University's School of Communications and Theater.

However, like most Black men who come from impoverished neighborhoods like North Philly, my story was more complicated than that. It was influenced by the ills that were thrust on my community, and my own poor decisions made things worse. Addiction had almost killed me more than once, and in living through that trauma, I'd already beaten the odds.

The job was supposed to be the next step in my comeback, and though I'd previously started over after losing everything, this time was going to be different. This change was going to be permanent. But now my mugshot was on television, and since there was no TV at my desk, I didn't even know it. That is, until the phone rang.

I picked up and listened with growing dread as a friend explained that he'd seen me on television. They were saying I had bench warrants, that I was one of Philadelphia's most wanted.

I remember my throat going dry and my heart racing wildly, but I don't know what I said to him in response. I only recall feeling the intense fear of being trapped as I hung up the phone. Then I dialed the one person I believed could help.

"Mom," I said when she answered the phone. "They showed me on the news. They said I have bench warrants. What should I do if somebody asks about it? I can't lose this job."

She paused, no doubt recalling all the times she'd told me to be honest, to tell the truth, to do all that I could to be an upstanding man. But in that moment she was afraid that all I'd done to change my life would be for naught.

My mother told me the only thing she could.

"Say it wasn't you," she said. "We'll figure out the rest later on."

After my mugshot blazed across television screens citywide, I waited for my shift at the front desk to end, half expecting the police to walk through the glass doors and arrest me. When they didn't, I went home knowing what I had to do.

I talked to the one person I trusted enough to advise me on what must come next, but even before my mother uttered the words, I knew the answer.

"You have to turn yourself in," she said.

I did, and my mother went with me.

It was an endless walk to the room where my fate would be decided. With each step, I felt a deep sense of foreboding, like everything I'd done on the streets of Philadelphia was waiting for me on the other side of the door.

I could feel the beads of sweat popping out on my forehead as my heart beat against my chest. My breathing was shallow and my eyes were unfocused. I couldn't see what was in front of me. All I could see was a past I dragged behind me like a heavy weight. It slowed me down as I walked through the door, but once I made it to the other side, something clicked, and though I'd struggle a few times more, I knew then that addiction wouldn't destroy me.

That was twenty-six years ago.

After each of my cases was dropped, I walked into a future I couldn't have imagined back then, but even now, I'm worried about sharing the details of my past. Will the world view me differently when they learn of my lengthy arrest record? Will it matter when they hear how far I fell during my struggle with drugs? Will they care that I was never convicted of any crime?

I honestly don't know, but I'm sure I have no refuge other than truth, and the truth is, I'm not the only one who suffered during the height of the War on Drugs. The entire Black community was stripped of everything, even to the point of death.

1

GEORGE FLOYD

WHY WE DEMAND REPARATIONS

WHEN I SAW THE VIDEO OF GEORGE FLOYD DYING AT THE hands of Minneapolis police, I thought of the night I spent panicked that I would be locked up for outstanding bench warrants. Like me, George called out to his mother, but when he did so, there was no answer. Instead, there was a knee on his neck and cuffs on his wrists, and though none of us knew it at the time, there was also the weight of a burgeoning movement on his back.

It's a movement that's driven not just by one death, but by the cumulative and deadly effects of a criminal justice system steeped in white supremacy. That system's racist goals are not new. They were born in the womb of chattel slavery, nurtured in the arms of Jim Crow, and ushered into adulthood by America's War on Drugs.

America must now right the wrongs of a past that is littered with laws meant to subjugate African Americans. Almost from our country's inception, slave codes monitored the movement of the enslaved, forbade them from owning guns, or learning to read, or gathering in groups without their enslaver's permission. After emancipation, Black codes continued the gun restrictions, adding vagrancy laws that made it illegal for African Americans to be unemployed, and other laws that kept Blacks from serving on juries.

These laws and many that followed set the precedent for the modern-day drug laws that similarly target Black people. The groups that enforced them served as the predecessors to today's police.

Now the War on Drugs serves as a sort of proxy for Black codes, disproportionately punishing Blacks even when they engage in behavior that is similar to that of their white counterparts.

For example, Reagan-era mandatory minimums racially targeted Blacks by creating a hundred-to-one difference in sentencing for crack versus powder cocaine.[1] Even after the disparity was reduced to eighteen-to-one by the Obama administration's Fair Sentencing Act, the damage was already done.[2] According to the late US Representative John Conyers, a Michigan Democrat who pushed for the sentencing change, Reagan's mandatory minimums increased the number of drug offenders in federal prisons from less than five thousand in 1980 to almost a hundred thousand by 2009.

However, crack isn't the only issue. There are also racial disparities in marijuana arrests, and according to the American Civil Liberties Union, those disparities exist in every state, across counties, and in places where the Black population is large and small. In other words, it can't be explained by anything other than race, and it hasn't disappeared as state restrictions on marijuana have loosened.

Even after marijuana was legalized for recreational or medical use in eleven states and the District of Columbia, the racial disparities in arrests remained. On average, a Black person is still 3.64 times more likely to be arrested for marijuana possession than a white person.[3] This, despite the fact that Black and white people use marijuana at about the same rates.

That's a dangerous truth for African Americans, because once they're in custody, the Sentencing Project says Blacks are more likely to be charged, more likely to be convicted, and more likely to face longer sentences than their white counterparts.

Sadly, Blacks are also more likely to have their life chances deeply impacted by criminal records. That's a truth George Floyd must have known all too well.

Raised by a single mother who moved to Houston from North Carolina when he was a toddler, George Floyd grew up in Cuney Homes, a public housing complex in Houston's Third Ward, a mostly Black area of the city. But he was more than the place he came from, more than the poverty that existed there, and more than the symbol he would later become. He was a human being, and his name was George.

A good athlete, George attended Jake Yates High School, where he starred in basketball and football. He went on to play basketball for two years at a Florida community college, and in 1995, he spent a year at Texas A&M University in Kingsville.

Despite his height—he was six feet seven—and his obvious athletic ability, his basketball career wasn't panning out, so he went back to live with his mother in Houston's Cuney Homes. He found work in security and construction.

Like many Black communities across the country, Cuney Homes was overpoliced, and George was sometimes caught up in police sweeps when he lived there. It didn't help that he was in Texas, where the War on Drugs is very much alive.

George was arrested nine times over the course of ten years, mostly for minor drug possession or theft cases, usually serving a few months at a time in jail. Once, he was arrested and jailed for fifteen days for failing to identify himself to a police officer. In his most serious case, which was also his last, George pleaded guilty to aggravated robbery with a deadly weapon. He was sentenced to five years and was paroled after four.

Just as we've seen in other cases of police violence against Black people, George's prior police record was used as a veritable sledgehammer by those who want to believe that Black victims deserve their fate.

Self-identified Black conservatives portrayed him as a thug who was beneath our community's respect. Police union presidents said his criminal record was purposely being concealed from the public. In truth, though, George Floyd's record was much more than a reflection of who he was. It was an indication of who he still had a chance to be. I firmly believe that, because my history is similar to his.

Like George Floyd, I am a Black man who grew up in an impoverished urban community. Like him, I used drugs and was arrested more than half a dozen times. Like him, I am a father who has had to start over more than once, and while there are major differences between us, the only one that matters is that I am alive to tell our stories.

George Floyd could have been any Black man in any major city in America. He grew up in a community where police were like an occupying force. He made some mistakes like all of us do. He lived in a state where the War on Drugs made him more likely than whites to be arrested.

Yet even as statistics can explain George Floyd's past, nothing can explain what happened to him six years after he decided to leave Houston to start a new life in Minneapolis.

The incident that led to George's death began around 8 p.m. on Monday, May 25, 2020, when a store owner accused George of passing a counterfeit twenty-dollar bill.

When store employees couldn't settle the dispute, police were called. Minutes later, George was approached by a Black officer and a white officer as he sat in a sport utility vehicle near the store. As a witness parked behind them filmed the exchange, one officer pulled a gun and ordered George to place his hands on the steering wheel. Then, after holstering the weapon, the officer grabbed George by the arm and dragged him out of the driver's seat.

Video of the incident shows that George's face was twisted into something approaching anguish as the officers pushed him across the sidewalk and sat him against a wall. As officers questioned him, George repeatedly called them "Sir," and while officers openly wondered if he was on some kind of drug, George continually assured them that he was cooperating.

They placed him in a police car and George complained that he was claustrophobic. They dragged him across the vehicle's backseat and he fell onto the street. That's where three officers knelt on his back, legs, and neck. A fourth officer sought to keep onlookers at bay as some of them, including a teenage girl named Darnella Frazier, watched and filmed the confrontation on their phones. Voices from the crowd begged Officer Derek Chauvin to remove his knee from George's neck, and as all of this was happening, George repeatedly cried out that he couldn't breathe.

For anyone with an ounce of humanity, it's difficult to watch videos of the incident that show Chauvin continuing to press his knee into George's neck for nine minutes and twenty-nine seconds, prompting an increasingly panicked George to call out to his deceased mother and to his children. Even in the midst of George's cries for mercy, Chauvin refused to let him get up, and according to transcripts from police body cameras, the officers wondered again if George was under the influence of a controlled substance.

As the minutes ticked by, George pleaded for help as he struggled to breathe with Chauvin's knee against his neck. "I'm through. I'm through," George said. "I'm claustrophobic. My stomach hurts. My neck hurts. Everything hurts. Can I get some water or something, please? Please? I can't breathe, officer."[4]

"Then stop talking, stop yelling," Chauvin said. "It takes a heck of a lot of oxygen to talk."

At that, George once again begged for his next breath. "Come on, man. Oh, oh. I cannot breathe. I cannot breathe. Ah! They'll kill me. They'll kill me. I can't breathe. I can't breathe. Oh!"

Bystanders grew irate, shouting and cursing at Chauvin to remove his knee from George's neck as the Black man's shouts became whimpers, as his whimpers faded to gasps, and as his voice was ultimately silenced. About five minutes after Officer Chauvin pushed his knee into George Floyd's neck, George lay motionless and unresponsive, according to trial testimony that was later provided by pulmonologist Martin J. Tobin.[5]

Genevieve Hansen, a white off-duty firefighter and EMT, happened upon the scene and saw that George was in distress—his face smashed against the asphalt as his bladder emptied in the street. She asked if she could check his pulse but was told by Officer Tou Thao to stand back, according to Hansen's trial testimony. Chauvin's knee remained on George's neck, Hansen kept asking to check his pulse, and her requests were repeatedly denied. When paramedics arrived and managed to get Chauvin to move his knee, they loaded George into an ambulance. After repeated attempts to resuscitate him, he was finally moved to a hospital, where he was pronounced dead.

Minneapolis police officers murdered George Floyd—a fact that was confirmed when a jury found Derek Chauvin guilty of second-degree unintentional murder, third-degree murder, and second-degree manslaughter. It was a crime that was captured by multiple cameras—a crime that played out in agonizing detail on our phones, computers, and televisions. It was a crime that was denounced from the streets of America's cities to the halls of power, where President Joe Biden showed tremendous growth from his days as the author of the 1994 Crime Bill and, in 2021, denounced systemic racism for what it is. Yet the War on Drugs, and the anti-Black bigotry that undergirds it, allowed some to try to justify Chauvin's unspeakable act of violence.

Toxicology reports revealed that George, a father of five who was fiercely loved by his family, had traces of fentanyl, methamphetamine, and marijuana in his system when he died. Blaming the drugs for George's death was the foundation of Chauvin's failed defense strategy at his murder trial. But for much of white America, regardless of political or social ideology, the response to Black drug use is often driven by racism.

Conservative whites seized on George Floyd's drug use to malign him. Moderate whites used it as justification for the officers who killed him. Progressive whites, while they saw George as a victim and approved of

Chauvin's murder conviction, still nevertheless save their greatest advocacy for largely white opioid users.

And, while it's true that thousands upon thousands of outraged whites risked their very lives to take to the streets and protest George Floyd's death, it's also true that even some of the most liberal whites have learned to ignore Black suffering when it comes to America's drug use.

The simple truth is that Black crack addicts are cast as enemies in a War on Drugs while white heroin addicts are the victims in an opioid crisis. It is why white America didn't want to see addiction as a medical issue until 2016, the year that nearly 80 percent of Americans who died from heroin and similar drugs were white.[6] It is why police officers pin Black men like George Floyd down when they believe they are under the influence, while cops are trained to administer Narcan so they can save white drug users' lives.

The racism of the War on Drugs has made America comfortable with the dehumanization of Black people. It is a brand of racism that has advanced to the point where jailing Blacks is no longer enough. Now we are simply killed.

However, with white faces now defining America's opioid overdose epidemic, the problem has been rebranded, and whites who were silent during the Black crack crisis have suddenly recognized drug abuse as a national emergency.

I call it the gentrification of addiction.

White progressives who had no problem referencing Black people as "addicts" want to remove that word from our lexicon and instead refer to addiction using its gentrified name—"substance use disorder."

Heroin must no longer be referred to by its traditional name. Instead, it's just another opioid. Helping an addict use drugs is no longer called "enabling." It's now lumped in under the phrase "harm reduction."

In fact, it is in the name of harm reduction that government officials in Philadelphia, San Francisco, and several other cities are working with various entities to open so-called safe injection sites so that addicts can shoot drugs under the watchful eye of doctors.

This, even though federal law says: "It shall be unlawful to knowingly open, lease, rent, use, or maintain any place, whether permanently or temporarily, for the purpose of manufacturing, distributing, or using any controlled substance."

The response to that, which is bathed in white liberal racism, is that the federal law in question was meant to apply only to crack houses. Which means it was supposed to apply only to Black people.

But if it is now legal to help addicts use drugs at a government-sanctioned site, Black people who had their property, their freedom, and their humanity taken during the War on Drugs must now receive reparations.

The Black community must be made whole, and not just for the War on Drugs but also for America's ongoing war on the humanity of Black people.

The criminal justice system has been unbothered by that reality. In fact, the system benefited from the chaos. In Philadelphia alone, the District Attorney's Office, through its Civil Asset Forfeiture Program, seized cash, cars, and homes from people who were accused of being involved in the drug trade.

Between 2002 and 2014, at least $72 million in cash and possessions were taken from those alleged to have been involved in dealing drugs and other crimes.[7] Many were Black, and some were never charged. The assets went directly to the DA's office, which ran the program. That was a clear conflict of interest, but the program was not widely questioned. That changed years later in 2014, when Christos Sourovelis, a white man, joined with several other plaintiffs to file a class-action suit after the city of Philadelphia tried to take his family's house after his son sold forty dollars' worth of drugs outside his home without the family's knowledge. With a white face out front, the story went national. *Sourovelis v. City of Philadelphia* was settled in 2018.

However, Philadelphia was not unique. Governments at all levels in cities and states across America benefited from the War on Drugs through forfeiture programs and other means.

All of it was fed by addicts like me—people who worked and stole and lied and cheated to buy the drugs that made others rich. The criminalization of people like me has led to mass incarceration, with nearly 2.3 million people held in jails, prisons, and other detention facilities in America.[8] These prisoners are disproportionately Black and poor, and I was almost one of them, because in the eyes of the criminal justice system, Black lives don't matter.

That wrong must be rectified. Not only for the damage done to Black people by the War on Drugs, but also for the harm done to us by every racist law that preceded it. In truth, it is not just the actions of individuals and groups that fuel America's racist systems. It is America's laws.

And, while I am heartened by the fact that millions of people took to the streets to demand an end to racist policing in the wake of George Floyd's murder, I am also cognizant of the fact that effective protest must be accompanied by concrete goals, by very clear demands. Therefore, if America is going to move forward in its fight to change its racist criminal justice system, the country must do the same thing that I must do: tell the truth.

This must begin with addressing the most recent injury—the physical and financial harm Blacks have endured during the continuing War on Drugs.

As George Floyd's death so starkly reminded us, unarmed Blacks are three times more likely to be killed by police than their white counterparts.[9] That's a frightening prospect, given that the overpolicing of Black communities leads to more frequent encounters with law enforcement. In their paper "Racial Inequities in Drug Arrests: Treatment in Lieu of and after Incarceration," Barbara Ferrer and her coauthors assert that "research has found greater surveillance of and arrests related to illicit drug (e.g., crack cocaine) sales in markets that are more likely to have Black sellers than White sellers."[10]

In short, Blacks have been intentionally and systematically targeted by drug laws and by law enforcement, even though Blacks are no more likely to use or sell drugs than whites. With nearly three hundred thousand people imprisoned for drug crimes in 2018, and the Black rate of imprisonment nearly twice the rate as that of Hispanics and more than five times that of whites, Black communities have been decimated by the War on Drugs.[11]

The costs go well beyond mass incarceration. From asset forfeiture to broken families to lives taken in encounters with police, Blacks have lost too much to even begin to enumerate in this endless "war." There is no doubt that reparations are owed. The question is how to go about getting them.

Simply put, we can achieve reparations on a national scale by replicating the successful lawsuit against Philadelphia's Civil Asset Forfeiture Program. Though the suit yielded just $3 million for people whose property was unjustly taken or never returned, the verdict sets a precedent that should yield greater settlements for future claimants.

Organizations such as the American Civil Liberties Union are uniquely positioned to file such suits. With national reach and multiple offices, the ACLU has often joined with private firms to file suit against local governments over unconstitutional drug policies and practices. In fact, the ACLU's Criminal Law Reform Project is already examining the issue of civil asset forfeiture. In its explanation of such programs, the ACLU has said the property seizures, which benefit the very agencies that use them, are "motivated by profit rather than crime-fighting."[12]

Sourovelis v. City of Philadelphia has provided a road map for correcting that wrong, and if George Floyd's death served as the catalyst for reexamining such programs, then his sacrifice, at least, was not entirely in vain.

However, receiving reparations for the War on Drugs is simply the opening salvo in the battle for all that was unjustly taken from Black people over our centuries-long history in this country. We are owed for the stolen labor that built America. We are owed for the stolen property taken from Black farmers and others in the years after enslavement, notably in the sharecropping system that effectively forced Black citizens back into slavery. We are owed for the stolen lives that were taken through lynching and other race-related terrorism.

How to achieve it, though? In this, I am in agreement with Ta-Nehisi Coates, who identified the first step as the passage of the late congressman John Conyers's bill, HR 40, which calls for the study of reparations to African Americans.

However, our fight will not be won solely by political means. Politics, after all, is the art of compromise, and on the issue of reparations, we must not compromise.

Our tactics must primarily be driven by capitalism—the same principle that drove America to abuse and exploit Black people from the moment we were brought to these shores. Money, after all, is the one thing America understands, and African Americans have $1.3 trillion in annual spending power.[13]

That financial power is our most potent weapon against America's recalcitrance, and we must use it with the kind of targeted proficiency that will force America to the table.

We must target corporate America with boycotts. In the spirit of Rev. Dr. Leon Sullivan, who used economics to force companies to hire Black workers, and later used the Sullivan Principles to force South Africa to abandon apartheid, Black Americans must withhold our money in order to build consensus for reparations.

To do this effectively, we must target one company at a time, and in addition to boycotting said company, we must engage in a maximum pressure campaign. That means targeting them with massive protests, calling them out on social media, canceling orders en masse, and doing it all to force them to the table as allies in the fight for reparations. It is corporate America, after all, that continues to benefit from the generational wealth enslaved workers created for whites. Therefore, corporate America, along with the federal government, must also be held accountable for the debt we are owed.

Black America must have financial reparations, because changing the racist structure of criminal justice in the future must begin with paying for its past.

THE DEMAND

We demand reparations. America must publicly admit what the numbers bear out: that its racist laws have consistently criminalized Black people, most recently through the War on Drugs, which continued a centuries-long pattern of stripping profit, property, and people from Black communities. America must then embark upon the financial repair of Black communities that have been damaged by legalized racism.

2

MICHAEL BROWN

THE CASE FOR CONSENT DECREES

IT WAS MIDDAY ON AUGUST 9, 2014, AND EIGHTEEN-YEAR-OLD Michael Brown and his friend Dorian Johnson were in Ferguson, Missouri, walking along Canfield Drive, a street that snakes through the Canfield Green apartment complex.

Michael's first cousin, Sabrina Webb, lived there, in one of the 414 units that Lipton Properties VII LP had renovated just a year before.[1] The investment in the community no doubt brought a sense of hope to a city that in just a generation had transformed from middle class to impoverished. Once a city where low-skilled job opportunities flourished for its mostly white residents, white flight made Ferguson a place where impoverished Blacks felt victimized by government officials, beginning with the police. And, while city officials like Mayor James Knowles, who is white, claimed Ferguson was a model of racial harmony, that was not the reality for Black people.

As a Justice Department investigation would later reveal, police officers in Ferguson were the first level of a system in which Black people were disproportionately stopped, ticketed, abused, and even jailed when they could not pay fines for minor offenses. Those fines were seen by many as a tool of oppression. But they were also a key government funding source in a city beset by poverty.

Located just north of St. Louis, Ferguson is a town of twenty-one thousand, where the unemployment rate had nearly tripled since 1990.[2] With economic and racial tensions a daily reality, relations between the mostly Black residents and the majority white police department were strained.

Perhaps that's why, when a white policeman named Darren Wilson pulled up in a police cruiser and spoke to Michael and his friend, both of whom were Black, the situation grew tense quickly.

By all accounts, the two young men were walking in the street on that mild summer day, and when Wilson stopped alongside and told them to get on the sidewalk, things escalated in mere seconds.

Dorian Johnson told investigators that when Wilson pulled up, the officer's cruiser was so close to Michael that when Wilson opened his car door, it bumped into the teenager. Dorian said that Wilson reached out of the car, grabbed Michael by the throat, and then clutched at Michael's shirt as the unarmed teen tried to move away. Dorian said he saw the officer draw a gun and shoot Michael in the chest or arm, and that Wilson hit Michael with another round as he was running away. According to Dorian, Wilson fired the fatal shots after Michael stopped and raised his hands in surrender.

Wilson, who did not initially give a public statement, had a different story, but the public didn't hear Wilson's version of events until much later, after his secret grand jury testimony was released.

Wilson claimed that Michael cursed at him after he asked the young men to stop walking in the street and that he tried to stop Michael because he matched the description from an earlier robbery report where a box of cigarillos was stolen from a store. Wilson said a scuffle ensued, and Michael, who was six feet five and 289 pounds, repeatedly punched and assaulted Wilson, who himself was six feet four and 210 pounds.

"When I grabbed him," Wilson told the grand jury, "the only way I can describe it is I felt like a five-year-old holding Hulk Hogan."[3]

Wilson said Michael tried to grab Wilson's gun, so Wilson fired through the car door. At that point, Wilson said, Michael looked at him with "the most intense aggressive face. The only way I can describe it, it looks like a demon."

Wilson said he fired again through his car door and Michael ran away. Wilson told the grand jury that he gave chase, and Michael stopped, turned around, and reached into his waistband while running toward the officer.

Wilson said he fired two series of shots and at one point saw Michael flinch as he continued to move toward the officer. "The face that he had was looking straight through me, like I wasn't even there," Wilson told the grand jury. Then Wilson described his version of Michael Brown's final moments.

"All I see is his head and that's what I shot," Wilson told the grand jury. "I saw the last one go into him. And then when it went into him, the demeanor on his face went blank, the aggression was gone. . . . The threat was stopped."

Wilson's testimony, predicated on the assertion that he feared for his life, was an echo of the same story police officers have relied on in similar cases. For Wilson, the threat began with two young Black men walking in the street. He claimed that Michael striking him in the face justified his use of deadly force. Wilson then told the grand jury that the threat to his life ended when he fired twelve rounds at an unarmed eighteen-year-old who in Wilson's eyes looked like a Hulk Hogan–sized demon.[4]

The Black community in Ferguson didn't see it that way. For them, the threat was the criminal justice system—from the police to the courts to the city government. As if to underline that point, law enforcement officials and other agencies in Ferguson allowed Michael's body to lie in the middle of Canfield Drive for four hours after he was killed by Darren Wilson.

The Ferguson Police Department, which claimed it lacked the resources and expertise to handle the case, almost immediately ceded the investigation to the St. Louis County Police Department. The county's homicide detectives were not called until about forty minutes after the shooting, and they didn't arrive at the scene until 1:30 p.m., according to county police logs. The medical examiner's investigator did not arrive at the scene until 2:30 p.m., and as investigators took pictures of the body, so did the residents.

A crowd began to gather at the edge of the yellow crime scene tape, and as the moments ticked by, people angrily denounced the police as murderers. Cops called for backup. Dogs were used to push back the crowd. However, as news of the shooting spread beyond Canfield Drive, the tension continued to build, and by the time Michael's relatives arrived, including his mother, Lesley McSpadden, the onlookers were livid. By 4 p.m., when Michael's body was removed from the street, the calls for protest had begun, and the racism of America's past met the white supremacy of its present.

For many in the Ferguson community and beyond, the delay in removing Michael's body from the street was reminiscent of a lynching in the Jim Crow era. It came across as a message.

"They shot a black man, and they left his body in the street to let you all know this could be you," Ferguson resident Alexis Torregrossa, twenty-one, told the *St. Louis Post Dispatch* in the weeks after the shooting. "To set an example, that's how I see it."[5]

That's how racial scholars see it too. In his 2015 study, "Two Nations, Revisited: The Lynching of Black and Brown Bodies, Police Brutality, and Racial Control in 'Post-Racial' Amerikkka," David G. Embrick of Loyola University explained how the treatment of Michael's body fit into America's racial narrative.

> It is not only the overt disregard for Black and brown lives that should offend us, it is also the spectacle of racial oppression—for example, the fact that Michael Brown's body was left on the street for hours after he was killed by police officer Darren Wilson—that points to just how little has changed in American race relations since the days of Jim Crow. In fact, race scholars such as Michael Omi, Howard Winant, Eduardo Bonilla-Silva, Joe R. Feagin, Michelle Alexander, and countless others have noted that one could look at modern day race practices (and the need for racial spectacle) as old perfume repackaged in a new bottle. Thus, the legitimacy given to police agencies represents a rearticulation of slavery and Jim Crow era practices specifically designed to socially control people of color. These modern day lynchings serve today in much the same way that they did in the past—as a way to illustrate and highlight white supremacy and emphasize minorities' place in a racialized social system.[6]

However, the shooting of Michael Brown and the misuse of his body as a racial spectacle had the opposite effect of Jim Crow–era lynchings. Rather than shrink into the darkness to quietly occupy some subordinate position in America's racial caste system, the residents of Canfield Drive used social media to highlight what happened. They called reporters and each other.

They texted and called relatives and friends, and as the news of Michael Brown's shooting spread, Dorian Johnson told all who would listen that his friend Michael had his hands raised in surrender when Darren Wilson fired the shots that killed him. It was Johnson's account, sincere and unrehearsed, that gave birth to the rallying cry around the murder of Michael Brown.

"Hands up! Don't shoot!" protesters shouted as they poured into the streets in Ferguson and in cities all over the world. But just as Michael's death at the hands of a police officer reanimated the Black Lives Matter movement, Michael's death also served as the catalyst for America's racist criminal justice system to protect itself from accountability.

The first tool the system used to quell dissent was violence. The second was an even more potent instrument, because it was cloaked in a veneer of justice. It's called the grand jury.

In the days and weeks after Michael Brown was shot to death by a cop, protesters poured into Ferguson's streets. They were met by police in military vehicles carrying weapons more suitable for the battlefield than for residential streets. As the pictures and videos of the militaristic police response filled the airwaves, so did the anger from communities across the country, including Philadelphia, where I was in my first days as a host on WURD Radio, the only Black-owned talk radio station in Pennsylvania.

I fielded hundreds of calls from listeners who were livid at the police response to the demonstrations, incensed at the ongoing attempt to undermine the Black Lives Matter movement, and cynical about the prospects of Darren Wilson being charged and convicted in the shooting death of Michael Brown.

In truth, Black people had every reason to suspect that the system would find a way to exonerate Wilson. As a police officer, Wilson was part of a politically connected brotherhood so deeply entrenched that its enablers exist at every level, even in the district attorney's offices that are frequently charged with investigating police shootings. District attorneys are most often elected officials, and they work closely with police to secure the convictions they need to win reelection. It is exceedingly rare for local prosecutors to charge police officers with shooting people on duty, because prosecutors are part of the law enforcement community. None more so than Bob McCulloch, who was the prosecuting attorney for St. Louis County at the time Michael Brown was killed.

It's no surprise that McCulloch, who is white, worked closely with the police in Ferguson. He came from a family of police officers. His father was a policeman who was tragically killed in the line of duty when McCulloch was twelve. The assailant was a Black man, a fact that raised questions about McCulloch's ability to be impartial in a racially charged case like Michael Brown's.

McCulloch's mother, uncle, brother, and cousin also worked for the police department in St. Louis. In fact, McCulloch wanted to be a police officer himself but was unable to do so after a rare bone cancer caused him to have his leg amputated at the hip at the age of seventeen. McCulloch called being a prosecutor the next best thing.

However, McCulloch's relationship to policing was always there. Fourteen years before Michael was killed, two white officers from a countywide drug task force shot and killed Earl Murray and Ronald Beasley, two Black men who were both unarmed. While an FBI investigation raised questions about the officers' claim that Murray was driving toward police when they fired twenty-one bullets into Murray's car, a grand jury impaneled by McCulloch failed to indict the officers.

That history prompted Black political figures, including Missouri state senators Jamilah Nasheed and Maria Chapelle-Nadal and St. Louis County executive Charlie Dooley to demand that McCulloch step aside in favor of a special prosecutor. A Black attorneys' group called the Mound City Bar Association called for McCulloch to recuse himself.

Ultimately, McCulloch refused to do so. Instead, he impaneled a grand jury to investigate the shooting death of Michael Brown. McCulloch's decision stirred memories of the previous case and meant there would be no public process that would allow for witnesses to be questioned in open court. Rather, the proceedings would be cloaked in secrecy, and since grand juries hear only what the prosecutor places before them, McCulloch would shape the result. Even if the grand jury decided on an outcome that McCulloch didn't like, he was free to overrule them since the final decision to charge is up to the prosecutor.

However, the Michael Brown case did more than pit the will of Ferguson's impoverished Black community against the will of a prosecutor with deep ties to the police department. The shooting death of Michael Brown at the hands of a white officer pitted the entire American establishment against a grassroots protest movement called Black Lives Matter.

President Obama, after seeing the Ferguson Police Department's militaristic response to the group's protests, ordered a review of programs that enabled local law enforcement to buy military equipment. Obama also sent Attorney General Eric Holder to Ferguson to investigate the fatal shooting. By early September, as McCulloch's grand jury began the process of hearing seventy hours of testimony from sixty witnesses over the course of twenty-five days, the Black Lives Matter movement was gaining momentum with huge protests and sharp messaging driven largely by social media.[7]

The fight to control the narrative was about more than hashtags and images shared repeatedly online. It was also about mainstream media and the attempt to paint Michael as someone who deserved his fate. In the days after the shooting, that message was delivered in a grainy convenience store video that appeared to show Michael stealing cigarillos not long before Wilson shot him. The story was reported by various media outlets, including in this snippet from the *New York Times*: "Shortly before his encounter with Officer Wilson, the police say he was caught on a security camera stealing a box of cigars, pushing the clerk of a convenience store into a display case. He lived in a community that had rough patches, and he dabbled in drugs and alcohol. He had taken to rapping in recent months, producing lyrics that were by turns contemplative and vulgar."[8]

Though the *Times* passage is part of a larger story, it is awash in stereotypes that serve to make Michael Brown an unsympathetic character. The portrayals were much worse in right-wing media.

In the following quote from an article in the *New American*, titled "Ferguson's Michael Brown: The Tall Tale of the 'Gentle Giant,'" Michael was portrayed as a physically imposing criminal: "Brown certainly was a giant, as surveillance footage seems to prove, showing his 6'4", nearly 300-pound self towering over a petrified convenience-store employee, who got manhandled and intimidated for having the temerity to object to his store being robbed."[9]

Such portrayals aren't limited to Michael Brown. They are part of a pattern that is consistently applied to Black male victims. In their study titled "From 'Brute' to 'Thug': The Demonization and Criminalization of Unarmed Black Male Victims in America," researchers Calvin John Smiley and David Fakunle examine the phenomenon:

> There is a demonizing process that happens to unarmed Black men posthumously. Unlike earlier Black icons and figures, such as Dr. Martin Luther King, Jr. and Malcolm X, who were vilified while alive and then sanitized in death to be repackaged as an acceptable part of the United States historical narrative, these men are portrayed as thugs and criminals to seemingly justify their deaths while simultaneously shifting blame away from law enforcement.[10]

The irony in this case, and perhaps in many others, is that there were also stories to tell about Wilson, but they seemed to be shared far less frequently than the ones we heard about Michael Brown.

Before arriving in Ferguson, Darren Wilson had been fired from the Jennings, Missouri, Police Department, along with all of his fellow officers, because too many in the overwhelmingly white department were abusive to the city's mostly Black residents. However, Wilson had no problem finding another job in law enforcement. He simply had to go a few miles away, to Ferguson.

This was not unusual. In fact, Duke University's Ben Grunwald and John Rappaport of the University of Chicago examined the phenomenon in a paper for the *Yale Law Review* titled "The Wandering Officer." Grunwald and Rappaport studied ninety-eight thousand officers employed by five hundred agencies in the state of Florida and found a pattern:

> First, in any given year during our study, an average of just under 1,100 officers who were previously fired—three percent of all officers in the State—worked for Florida agencies. Second, officers who were fired from their last job seem to face difficulty finding work. When they do, it takes them a long time, and they tend to move to smaller agencies with fewer resources in areas with slightly larger communities of color. Interestingly, though, this pattern does not hold for officers who were fired earlier in their careers. Third, wandering officers are more likely than both officers hired as rookies and those hired as veterans who have never been fired to be fired from their next job or to receive a complaint for a "moral character violation." Although we cannot determine the precise reasons for the firings, these results suggest that wandering officers may pose serious risks, particularly given how difficult it is to fire a police officer.[11]

But as hard as it is to fire a police officer, it's also difficult to charge an officer with a crime when the system is rigged in his favor. By convening a grand jury to weigh the evidence against Darren Wilson, Robert McCulloch—the pro-police St. Louis County prosecutor—was effectively putting his thumb on the scales of justice.

While activists held fast to the "Hands up! Don't shoot!" mantra, and demonstrators engaged in "die-ins," lying on the ground for four minutes to symbolize the four hours that Michael's dead body lay on Canfield Drive, McCulloch's prosecutors seemingly worked on Wilson's behalf.

Records show that prosecutors aggressively questioned several grand jury witnesses who said Michael Brown's hands were up when Wilson shot him. That questioning was a harbinger of things to come.

With McCulloch leading the process, the grand jury declined to indict Darren Wilson for the death of Michael Brown.

The grand jury's decision, McCulloch said, turned on the testimony of witnesses who appeared to change their stories after publicly stating that Michael was killed with his hands up. McCulloch said some witnesses later admitted that they had not seen anything directly, adding that some witness statements were "completely refuted by the physical evidence."[12]

The prosecutor claimed that the biggest challenges to the investigation were social media rumors and the "the 24-hour news cycle and its insatiable appetite for something, for anything, to talk about." He snidely remarked that the grand jury's job was to "separate fact from fiction."[13]

Protesters across the country reacted with outrage. In Ferguson, peaceful demonstrations were punctuated by incidents of vandalism and looting. Over one thousand people marched in Manhattan. Hundreds more gathered in Oakland, Philadelphia, and Chicago, while an estimated three hundred gathered at the White House.

The night that the grand jury decision was announced, President Obama took to the airwaves to call for calm. But Black people and their allies wanted justice, and after Robert McCulloch failed to deliver, activists began a campaign that would eventually lead to his ouster after a twenty-eight-year reign as county prosecutor.[14] However, that didn't solve the issue of accountability for Michael Brown's death. The Justice Department was the last hope for that.

Throughout the grand jury process that led to Darren Wilson's acquittal, the Department of Justice was carrying out two parallel investigations. The first, which sought to determine if Wilson violated Michael Brown's civil rights when he shot and killed him, concluded with federal prosecutors declining to bring charges. In a statement, Justice Department prosecutors said they could not prove that "Wilson used unreasonable force when he shot Michael Brown and that he did so willfully, that is, knowing it was wrong and against the law to do so."[15]

That decision, which hinged on the Justice Department's claim that it could not meet the high standard of proof in federal civil rights cases, angered activists. But that rationale would be echoed many times in similar cases involving Black victims of police violence.

However, the second federal probe in the wake of Michael's death was a "pattern or practice" investigation of Ferguson's police department that uncovered the systemic racism undergirding the city's criminal justice system.[16] It led to the implementation of a consent decree—a powerful tool that can force reform when used correctly.

Consent decrees are binding agreements between local jurisdictions and the Department of Justice that mandate change in a police department. These agreements are made possible by a provision of the Violent Crime Control and Law Enforcement Act of 1994, the legislation more commonly known as the Crime Bill.

Typically, a consent decree is put in place after the Justice Department investigates and finds substantial evidence of "patterns of unlawful use of force; unlawful stops, searches and arrests; [or] racial discrimination."[17] Once that investigation is completed, a list of reforms is negotiated between the Justice Department, community members, and local officials. When the parties come to an agreement, a federal judge approves the consent decree and a federal monitor is assigned to oversee the reform process.

While each consent decree is slightly different based on what's found in the investigation, here is how they normally work: the consent decree lists the reforms that the city and police department must implement; the federal monitor keeps track of how and when the reforms are put in place; the affected community has input through an advisory board, public comments, or community forums; the federal judge holds regular court hearings to make sure the terms of the court order are being met.

In Seattle, for example, a consent decree was put in place after a 2012 Department of Justice investigation found a pattern of excessive force. The consent decree mandated "retraining of officers, modernizing all procedures related to the use of force including the reporting of incidents of officers using force."[18] It also called for the department to work closely with community representatives to change police methods and accomplish reform.

Five years into the agreement, Seattle's consent decree, which was overseen by Judge James Robart and monitored by attorney Merrick Bobb, both of whom are white, was successful in substantially reducing the department's use of force. Bobb issued a report that said as much.

That is how consent decrees are supposed to work, but the Justice Department's investigation of the Ferguson police uncovered a level of systemic racism that far outpaced what they found in Seattle.

In Ferguson, Justice Department investigators interviewed city officials, private citizens, police officers, and court officials; reviewed over thirty-five thousand pages of police records and thousands of emails; analyzed departmental data on stops, searches, citations and arrests; and went on police ride-alongs.[19] Their investigation found multiple examples of abuse, misconduct, and outright racism by the Ferguson Police Department. In a scathing 102-page report, the Justice Department outlined a few of them.

One example involved a Black man who told investigators that in August 2014, when he had an argument in his apartment, Ferguson police responded and pulled him out by force. "After telling the officer, 'you don't have a reason to lock me up,' he claims the officer responded: '[Nigger], I can find something to lock you up on.' When the man responded, 'good luck with that,' the officer slammed his face into the wall, and after the man fell to the floor, the officer said, 'don't pass out [motherfucker] because I'm not carrying you to my car.'"

In June 2014, a Black couple allowed their small children, who were playing in a park, to urinate in the bushes next to their parked car. According to the Justice Department report,

> An officer stopped them, threatened to cite them for allowing the children to "expose themselves," and checked the father for warrants. When the mother asked if the officer had to detain the father in front of the children, the officer turned to the father and said, "you're going to jail because your wife keeps running her mouth." The mother then began recording the officer on her cell phone. The officer became irate, declaring, "you don't videotape me!" As the officer drove away with the father in custody for "parental neglect," the mother drove after them, continuing to record. The officer then pulled over and arrested her for traffic violations. When the father asked the officer to show mercy, he responded, "no more mercy, since she wanted to videotape," and declared "nobody videotapes me." The officer then took the phone, which the couple's daughter was holding. After posting bond, the couple found that the video had been deleted.

Beyond the false arrests, physical abuse, and bigoted behavior, federal investigators found something even more troubling—a racist system driven by the same motivation that fueled America's original sin of slavery: money.

With a majority Black population and a white power structure controlling every aspect of city government, an apartheid system flourished in Ferguson. City Manager John Shaw, Mayor James Knowles, Chief of Police Thomas Jackson, municipal judge Ronald Brockmeyer, municipal court clerk Mary Ann Twitty, the city's prosecuting attorney, and every assistant court clerk were white, and according to the Justice Department, they worked together to fund Ferguson's government through fines and fees collected largely from Black residents.

In March 2010, the city's finance director wrote to police chief Thomas Jackson that "unless ticket writing ramps up significantly before the end of the year, it will be hard to significantly raise collections next year. . . . Given that we are looking at a substantial sales tax shortfall, it's not an insignificant issue." Then, in March 2013, the finance director wrote to the city manager: "Court fees are anticipated to rise about 7.5%. I did ask the Chief if he thought the PD could deliver 10% increase. He indicated they could try."

While Ferguson's inner circle was using fines and fees to victimize Black people, court clerk Mary Ann Twitty made sure powerful white people didn't face the same fate. Twitty fixed tickets at the request of the mayor, the police chief, and others, including municipal court judge Ronald Brockmeyer.

Meanwhile, Judge Brockmeyer personally created new court fees that were considered abusive and possibly unlawful, according to the Justice Department. "These include a $50 fee charged each time a person has a pending municipal arrest warrant cleared, and a 'failure to appear fine,' which the judge noted is 'increased each time the Defendant fails to appear in court or pay a fine.'"

The judge did not act alone. In fact, a February 2011 report noted that Brockmeyer said, "None of these changes could have taken place without the cooperation of the Court Clerk, the Chief of Police, and the Prosecutor's Office."

Overall, the Justice Department's report on Ferguson was so damning that municipal court judge Ronald Brockmeyer, city manager John Shaw, and chief of police Thomas Jackson all resigned, along with two Ferguson police officers who sent racist emails. Municipal court clerk Mary Ann Twitty was fired over similar emails.

Even with key players gone, the system remained in place, and after the Justice Department and city officials hammered out a deal for a consent decree enumerating specific reforms, Ferguson's city council tried to back out at the last minute. The Justice Department filed suit, and in March 2016, the Department of Justice and the City of Ferguson agreed to a consent decree designed to reform the patterns and practices uncovered by the federal investigation that followed the shooting death of Michael Brown.

Ferguson's 131-page consent decree mandates numerous reforms to overhaul the city's police and court systems. Among its requirements are reform of the Ferguson municipal code, community policing and engagement, municipal court reform, bias-free police and court practices, body-worn and in-car camera requirements for police, use of force standards, and officer training and support. Perhaps most importantly, it requires monitoring, compliance assessment, and enforcement.

As with all consent decrees, the success of Ferguson's agreement depends on the active and committed participation of several entities. These include the city's political and criminal justice leaders, the court-appointed federal monitor who tracks progress, the judge overseeing the agreement, and, most of all, the community.

That point was driven home to me when I spoke with former Justice Department attorney Sharon Brett. She was part of the team that carried out investigations and consent decree enforcement during the Obama and Trump administrations.

"Consent decrees are a vehicle," Brett told me in an interview.[20] "I don't know that they're perfect. I would not say that they're a perfect solution in every case, and I wouldn't say that they fix all problems exactly like they are intended to because a lot depends on really the culture of the department and the willingness of the leadership to make meaningful and lasting changes . . . In the jurisdictions where that leadership is not present it's a lot harder to see lasting change."

In Ferguson, lawyer and former police officer Natashia Tidwell leads the monitor team, which includes an African American studies professor, two community engagement consultants, police and technology experts, and an authority on white-collar crime and fraud. Their job, as the team describes it, is to "conduct reviews and audits to determine whether the City, Ferguson Police Department, and the Municipal Court are in compliance with the Consent Decree, and [to] provide technical assistance as needed to guide the City through the implementation process."[21]

But nearly five years into the process, while some written policies had been put in place to comply with the requirements of the consent decree, the Ferguson Police Department had not come up with training regimens that meet Department of Justice standards. In essence, "use of force" policies existed on paper, but Ferguson's officers had not received comprehensive training on many of those policies beyond what they heard at roll call.

"We're a small department," Ferguson police chief Jason Armstrong said during testimony at a consent decree status conference in January 2021. "We are understaffed, and we do not have a training coordinator. We do not have a dedicated training professional on this police department, and so we have people that have other duties and other responsibilities that also try to work on this training in addition to the other duties that they are fulfilling."[22]

In explaining why the training had not taken place, Armstrong told Judge Perry that additional issues including scheduling, staffing, and variation between state and Justice Department standards made it difficult to comprehensively train his officers on the new policies. His points were echoed by city lawyer Nicolle Barton.

But without true deadlines on implementing reforms, city officials can always provide excuses for why they can't complete the task. As with *Brown v. Board of Education*, the US Supreme Court ruling that required states to desegregate schools "with all deliberate speed," the vague time limits of consent decrees allow for such foot-dragging. That must end.

In the wake of Michael Brown's death, the consent decree was seen as a potent solution to force reform in rogue police departments. Today, even after one-time US attorney general Jeff Sessions sought to weaken them during the Trump years, these agreements remain in place, and as the fight for racial justice hits a new peak, consent decrees must be utilized to reform racist patterns and practices in police departments all over America. Since consent decrees were codified in the 1994 Crime Bill, which was authored by President Joe Biden when he was a US senator from Delaware, it now falls to Biden to toughen the standards of consent decrees, to set hard deadlines for change, and to do so while directly challenging racism in American law enforcement.

To do otherwise is a betrayal of the American people, because if we are to reform racist policing for Michael Brown and for all our children, consent decrees must be fully implemented.

THE DEMAND

Use consent decrees to reform police departments that demonstrate a "pattern or practice" of racism and police brutality and hold those departments accountable. Set hard deadlines for reform, implement clear penalties for noncompliance, and include real incentives to maintain community participation.

3
HASSAN BENNETT
THE CASE FOR COMPENSATION

THE ECHO OF GUNFIRE WAS A FAMILIAR SOUND IN THE streets of West Philly, but for Hassan Bennett, there was something decidedly more dangerous about the shots that rang out near Robinson and Lansdowne that day.

When he heard them, Hassan, who is Black, was at home on the phone. However, he knew that his friends were on that corner, and after hearing so many shots fill the autumn air, Hassan had to see if his friends were all right.

As he recounted the story to me in a radio interview nearly thirteen years after that fateful day, Hassan spoke as if it had occurred just recently.

"The female, Ms. Murray, that I was on the phone with, she was like, 'No don't go around there and check on your friends! What's wrong with you? Don't go around there. They're grown, they can handle themselves.' And I'm like, 'No, I gotta go around there and check on my friends.'"[1]

Hassan said he made several phone calls to see if his friends were all right. After they didn't answer, Hassan walked to the corner with mounting concern. Once there, he was met with carnage. His friend, nineteen-year-old Devon English, was dead, having been shot multiple times while sitting in a parked car with another friend, eighteen-year-old Corey Ford, who was to survive bullet wounds to his legs and buttocks.

Hassan said the police officers on the scene asked him if he knew someone named Lamont. "I said, 'I know a lot of Lamonts around here,'" Hassan recalled. "'You gotta be more specific.' Then he didn't have anything else, so I said, 'I don't have anything for you,' and they walked away."

That was September 22, 2006. A sixteen-year-old named Lamont Dade was arrested for the shooting. Three days later, Hassan was too. According to police, the motive for the shooting was twenty dollars that Hassan allegedly lost to Devon English in a dice game. Their working theory was that Hassan was the mastermind behind the shooting, and that he enlisted the younger Dade to help him carry it out.

When the case went to trial, Hassan testified, while his co-defendant, Dade, did not. Corey Ford, the surviving victim, offered his testimony, saying that Hassan was not the shooter.

"[Corey] testified that I didn't do it," Hassan said. "He said my co-defendant and another guy did it. And they presented a letter and [Corey] said the same thing in the letter.

"I didn't know much law in my first trial," Hassan said. "But I don't have to touch a stove to know I'm being burnt by it—to know I shouldn't be touching the stove. So, the feeling I got when the first trial came about—as the first trial was [winding] up—it wasn't a feeling like I'm winning. I didn't know nothing, but it wasn't a feeling like I'm winning."

In the end, though, Hassan never found out how the jury was going to rule. The proceedings ended in a mistrial due to alleged jury tampering by the defense.

Hassan explained it this way: "What had happened—how the first trial ended—the first trial ended in a mistrial because one of the juror's neighbors told her, 'Listen, from what I hear in the neighborhood, Hassan didn't do it.' The juror then went and told the judge, and the judge declared it a mistrial."

But later that year, when his retrial took place, things were decidedly different.

Unlike in the first trial, Hassan's co-defendant took the stand and testified against him. Ford, the surviving witness, changed his story to implicate Hassan as the shooter. There was also a jailhouse snitch who testified that Hassan admitted in jail that he had committed the shooting.

Although a close family friend corroborated Hassan's testimony—that he was in the house when the crime occurred—that wasn't enough. After three days of deliberation, the jury came back with a guilty verdict.

"They decided to find me guilty of second-degree murder, possession of an instrument of crime, aggravated assault, and criminal conspiracy," Hassan told me. "I was sentenced to life in prison, plus 8 to 40 for the conspiracy, 2-and-a-half to 5 for the possession of an instrument of crime, and for the aggravated assault I was sentenced to 5 to 10."

Two days later, on Christmas Eve 2008, Hassan was transferred from a city jail to a state correctional institution to begin serving his sentence. As the prison doors shut behind him, Hassan was left in disbelief.

"The thoughts that's going through my mind is I'm living, but I'm not living," Hassan told me. "I'm living outside my body, if that makes any sense. I feel like I'm drowning. I'm going through the motions, but this isn't me. All I can think about is, 'Yo, I got life. I got life.'"

Hassan Bennett, one of countless innocent African Americans imprisoned in the United States, was just beginning his yearslong ordeal in the criminal justice system. Racism played a role in his false imprisonment, but Hassan's case was also emblematic of another systemic issue that tends to fly under the radar: police misconduct.

African Americans convicted of murder or sexual assault are far more likely than whites to later be found innocent of the crimes, according to the National Registry of Exonerations.

A 2017 study looked at thirty years of data and found that Black people, who make up about 13 percent of the US population, account for 50 percent of those wrongfully convicted of murder.[2] To make matters worse, these wrongfully convicted Blacks stay an average of three more years in prison than whites in similar circumstances.

"It's no surprise that in this area, as in almost any other that has to do with criminal justice in the United States, race is the big factor," Samuel Gross, a University of Michigan law professor and a senior editor of the registry, told the *New York Times*.

Wrongful convictions are indeed a common occurrence, especially where African Americans are concerned. However, these miscarriages of justice don't take place in a vacuum. They happen in concert with the other racial disparities that exist at every stage of the criminal justice system.

That's why the Sentencing Project's 2018 report to the United Nations is relevant at nearly every stage of the criminal justice system. Blacks are more likely to be arrested and convicted and to face harsher sentences than whites.

In essence, the African American path to wrongful conviction begins with the racial disparities in arrests, and those unwarranted arrests are helped along by the utter disregard for the humanity of Black suspects.

In cases where even a cursory review of the evidence should give the authorities pause, Black suspects are denied the benefit of the doubt, and they are often thrust into a criminal justice system that is eager to convict them at all costs.

This is true in states across the nation. That's why Hassan Bennett faced life in prison for a crime he didn't commit in Pennsylvania, and why, in Texas, a Black man named Anthony Graves was wrongfully convicted and sentenced to death.

Graves's story began in 1992 when a Black man named Robert Carter used a pistol, hammer, and knife to kill six members of a family, including Carter's two-year-old son. Carter set a fire to try to cover up his crime, and when he was questioned by police, Carter lied and said Graves was involved.

Police interrogated Graves for hours without a lawyer present, misled him about the results of a lie detector test, and placed Graves in a cell across from Carter, the actual murderer, in the hopes that Graves would say something to incriminate himself. When he didn't, a jailer simply made something up at trial—falsely testifying that he heard Graves tell Carter that he'd done "the job" for him.[3] But while police told lies in an attempt to build a case against Graves, their actions paled in comparison to the egregious misconduct of the prosecutor who tried the case.

Charles Sebesta, a white man who was then the district attorney for Burleson County, Texas, went to trial with a case based solely on the testimony of Carter, who made repeated attempts to recant his statement that Graves was involved in the crime. Sebesta failed to inform the jury or defense counsel of this exculpatory evidence during Graves's trial, even though he was required to do so by constitutional and ethical rules. Sebesta also coerced Carter into again identifying Graves as his accomplice during trial by threatening to prosecute Carter's wife for the crime. But Sebesta didn't stop there. He kept an alibi witness from testifying at trial by threatening to make her a suspect in the murders.

Sebesta's misconduct was so brazen and unethical that he was eventually disbarred for it, but not before Graves spent eighteen years in prison, including a dozen years on death row.

Graves wrote letters to maintain his sanity, connecting with allies around the globe—allies who fought to help Graves win his freedom. In the years since he was freed in 2015, Graves penned a book called *Infinite Hope: How Wrongful Conviction, Solitary Confinement, and 12 Years on Death Row Failed to Kill My Soul.*

Graves was eventually freed because lawyers and a journalism professor worked tirelessly to gather evidence and file appeals on his behalf. He was freed because he refused to give in to the notion that he should lose his life—either through the cruelest form of imprisonment, solitary, or the death penalty—for a crime he didn't commit.

Anthony Ray Hinton, who was wrongfully convicted in Alabama, was similarly insistent concerning his innocence. Arrested and charged with two counts of capital murder at just twenty-nine, Hinton was poor, African American, and subject to a different criminal justice system than whites in the South. Oh sure, it looked the same on the surface, but for Blacks, it functioned differently. Hinton knew that, and for his first three years on death row, he was filled with all the rage one would expect. But over time, he began to realize that he could do and be something more. He ran a book club on death row, and in doing so he convinced killers and thieves and racists to talk about things that mattered.

Hinton shared a snippet from one of those conversations in his book, *The Sun Does Shine*. In the passage, Hinton and a group of men on death row, including a racist convicted of lynching a Black boy, discuss the racism depicted in James Baldwin's *Go Tell It on the Mountain*. As they talk about the futility of hatred, Hinton speaks up.

"We are all God's children, and this world belongs to all of us," he says. "I know the sun will never refuse to shine. We may not see it, but I know it's there. I'm not going to have hate in my heart. I spent some dark years here with nothing but hate in my heart. I can't live like that."[4]

Hinton's change of heart was a personal decision to choose love over hate, despite being the victim of a system that clearly hated him. That choice was necessary for his own well-being, but it wound up affecting everyone around him, including a lawyer named Bryan Stevenson who founded the Equal Justice Initiative to challenge mass incarceration, excessive punishment, and racial and economic injustice. As an impoverished Black man trapped in Alabama's racist criminal justice system, Hinton was among the vulnerable that Stevenson sought to represent. However, it was Hinton and others, like the wrongfully convicted Walter McMillian, who inspired Stevenson.

Wrongfully convicted for killing a young white woman, McMillian was the subject of Stevenson's bestselling book, *Just Mercy*, which also included the stories of Hinton and others. Adapted into a film starring Michael B.

Jordan and Jamie Foxx, *Just Mercy* told the uplifting story of a man who escaped a system meant to kill him. But it also exposed something far more insidious.

Just Mercy exposed the death penalty as the bastard son of lynching. Born of a racist justice system that targets African Americans just as surely as the white mobs of the not-so-distant past, state-sanctioned capital punishment lends an air of credibility to the brutal act of killing Black people. But law does not equal justice, especially where the death penalty is concerned.

In 2017, the NAACP reported that while Black people comprised 13 percent of the US population, Blacks accounted for 42 percent of inmates on death row in both state and federal prison systems. And, in state prisons, Blacks were 35 percent of those who were actually executed.[5] But the racism that is so prevalent in the application of the death penalty is not just about the race of the defendant. It is also about the race of the victim. In their 2020 study, "Whom the State Kills," researchers found that the execution rate for defendants sentenced to the death penalty was seventeen times higher when the victim was white than when the victim was Black.[6]

In short, if America's prison system were a sundown town, the death penalty would be the hand-lettered sign warning Blacks not to be caught there after dark.

Anthony Graves, Anthony Ray Hinton, Walter McMillian, and so many other African Americans decided to love, grow, and change in spite of being stuck in the dark. We are inspired by that, and also by the families, community members, activists, and lawyers who help such people to win their freedom.

However, when wrongful convictions are undergirded by willful police misconduct and lawyers only serve to make matters worse, it is sometimes necessary to find other light within the darkness.

That's what Hassan Bennett did when he was wrongfully convicted of killing his friend and wounding another man in West Philly. In the prison where he was mandated to endure a life sentence, Hassan found light in the hole.

In the winter of 2008, after being sentenced to life for killing one of his friends and wounding another, Hassan was in a state of shock. The only thing he knew was that he couldn't allow the conviction to stand.

"So, I'm trying to fight," he told me in our radio interview. "The only way I know how is through the law library. I'm trying to go up there and go in the law library. But for my first couple of years it was like going through the motions. I had a very hard time in the state correctional facility 'cause a lot of times they would tell me to do things and I would be like, 'I'm not even supposed to be here. Why do I have to do that? I'm not even supposed to be here.'

"And they would be like, 'Man, just do it!'

"And I'm like, 'No, I'm not doing it 'cause I'm not even supposed to be here.' I spent a lot of time in the hole in the state correctional institution. Sometimes I just went to the hole 'cause I didn't want to deal with the state correctional institution and the law library services were better in the hole than they were on population."

In the hole—better known as solitary confinement—inmates were allowed to keep materials from the law library for three weeks at a time, Hassan said. Under normal circumstances, inmates could only visit the law library for three to four hours at a time. So, in some ways, the punishment of solitary confinement provided solace for Hassan. At the same time, it gave him the opportunity to study the law like never before.

Still, Hassan's interest in fighting for his freedom waxed and waned. He sometimes experienced bouts of hopelessness, and at one point, he adopted a routine at the prison. Studying the law wasn't part of it.

"I began to fall into what's known as a bid," Hassan told me. "That's your place in jail, what you do to pass time. In jail they tell you, 'Do the time. Don't let the time do you.' Well, I began to let the time do me for like a good six months."

That is, until a man named Prince, from Harlem, New York, took Hassan aside and talked to him about going back to the law library to resume his fight for exoneration. Prince reminded him that he'd learned the rules of evidence and how to write petitions and motions. He reminded Hassan that he wasn't there just to do a bid.

"And I went and got back in the law library and I went deep," Hassan said. "I went and studied everything. I read every book I got my hands on."

For nearly six years, Hassan read books, law journals, newspapers, and legal briefs. He read enough to master the intricacies of the law, and by 2014, he needed every bit of that knowledge to challenge the questionable actions of the lawyer who represented him.

"On October 3, 2014, Attorney Earl Kaufmann, who I had at the time, sent me a letter saying the judge was getting ready to deny my PCRA petition," Hassan explained. "Now, a PCRA petition is [the] Post Collateral Relief Act. It's asking the lower court judge, 'Listen, I have evidence that proves I am wrongfully convicted of a crime I didn't commit or I was illegally sentenced.' Those are the only two ways you can get in on a PCRA. I filed it under I was wrongfully convicted of a crime I didn't commit."

Hassan said his lawyer hadn't filed the petition properly, so Hassan stepped in to advocate for himself, filing the petition for himself, and repeatedly writing to the judge to tell her that the lawyer wasn't doing his job. In response, the judge granted Hassan a Grazier hearing, a court proceeding that determines whether the defendant validly waived his right to counsel during a PCRA hearing and ensures that the defendant is waiving his right knowingly, voluntarily, and intelligently.

Hassan's PCRA petition was approved, winning him a new trial, and at the Grazier hearing, he won the right to represent himself. The wins gave him the confidence to begin preparing for the third trial. He immediately got to work.

"I'm writing questions for every witness," he recalled of his days of preparation. "It's been two trials and I have statements. I have discovery. I have everything they have. So I'm writing questions. And I already got the answers that I want. You already answered it in another trial. So if you don't answer that way, then I can direct your attention [to previous statements]."

That's exactly what he did. He asked questions for which he already knew the answers, trapping the prosecution's witnesses, including the detectives who worked on his case, whenever they contradicted their previous testimony. The tactic almost worked. The panel came back having voted eleven to one for acquittal, resulting in a hung jury and setting the stage for a fourth and final trial.

Hassan came to the fourth trial having made a fateful decision. There had already been enough lies, he thought, so Hassan walked into the courtroom and pleaded his case while wearing his prison uniform. When I asked him why he did that, his answer was simple.

"Why lie?" Hassan asked rhetorically. "Why disguise? If I put on a disguise in front of you, I'm hiding something. If you figure out I'm hiding something, if it looks like I'm hiding something, how can you trust what's coming out of my mouth? I'm just a tricky lawyer if I show you I'm hiding something."

The effect of Hassan's prison clothing was jarring, but it was his command of the facts that influenced the outcome, especially when it came to the police misconduct that led to his conviction.

Hassan told the jury that former Philadelphia homicide detective James Pitts coerced shooting survivor Corey Ford and Lamont Dade, Hassan's co-defendant, into giving incriminating statements against Hassan. That was not an unusual allegation. Pitts had a long record of being accused of using coercion and even physical abuse to force false confessions from witnesses and defendants. According to a 2017 report from the *Philadelphia Inquirer*, the City of Philadelphia paid or was ordered to pay more than $2.5 million in seven lawsuits in which Pitts was named as a defendant.

Hassan filed a motion to present Pitts's history to the jurors. The district attorney argued against it and the judge denied the motion. That meant Hassan wasn't allowed to say anything about the many lawsuits and allegations of Pitts forcing confessions.

Still, there was no doubt that the witnesses changed their stories over time. Both Corey Ford's and Lamont Dade's initial statements said that Dade shot Devon English and rifled his pockets, and that Hassan shot Ford numerous times. The men recanted their statements in court, testifying that Pitts forced them to identify Hassan as the shooter. When Hassan called Pitts to the stand, the former detective claimed the men were lying, but Hassan challenged Pitts on his testimony. The jury believed Hassan, even without testimony about the numerous lawsuits, court filings, and Internal Affairs reports in which Pitts has been accused of forcing statements from suspects and witnesses in other cases.

As a result, Hassan was acquitted on all counts and released from prison. Weeks after that triumphant moment, as he sat before me in a radio studio, I asked Hassan what he felt when he was freed.

"Vindication. Certification. Like, 'Yes! I'm here! I proved it!' I not only proved that I didn't do this crime. I proved that we ain't as dumb as you think we are. When we put our mind to something we can accomplish anything. It ain't nothing that we can't accomplish once we dedicate our mind to it and find the resources to get it done."

Hassan, who has often spoken publicly concerning issues of police racism and misconduct since his release, now works with the Defender's Association of Philadelphia, helping others who are accused of crimes.

However, Hassan's story is not complete, because he has not received recompense for the nearly thirteen years he lost to a racist criminal justice system. Pennsylvania is one of fifteen states that provides no compensation for those who've been wrongly imprisoned, and that's unjust.

In addition, after numerous complaints and millions paid out by taxpayers to settle lawsuits stemming from forcibly coerced confessions, James Pitts has not been fired. As of February 2021, he was still employed with the Philadelphia Police Department, and that is an outrage.

To echo the words from Hassan Bennett's closing statement at his final trial, "We can't tolerate this misconduct. We can't tolerate these actions."

I agree, and therefore we must move to make things right.

Working tirelessly to demand repair for the damage done by a system that would steal years from a life and give nothing in return requires a special kind of daring. We have seen that level of fortitude from nonprofit entities that continue to fight this battle.

Among them is the Innocence Project, which is calling for all fifty states to compensate those who have been wrongfully convicted. According to their research, thirty-five states currently do so. However, the compensation is not uniform, and in many cases, there are restrictions that prevent the exonerated from receiving anything.

This is unfortunate, because the wrongfully convicted face difficulties after they are exonerated while attempting to build a life outside of prison. With no recent work history or credit history, their prospects of securing something as basic as safe and affordable housing are slim. And their unfamiliarity with new technologies presents challenges as well. At the very least, the wrongfully convicted are in need of technical assistance upon their release. In practical terms, however, they are owed much more than that.

The baseline for compensation should begin with the list of requirements laid out by the Innocence Project in an online petition seeking support for the wrongfully convicted. They include "monetary compensation at a fixed rate for each year served in prison; the immediate provision of subsistence funds; and access to critical services such as housing, food, psychological counseling, medical/dental care, job skills training, education, and other relevant assistance needed to foster the successful rebuilding of their lives."[7]

Developing a national policy around compensation for the wrongfully convicted will require more than an online petition, however. It will require legislation. That means working on the municipal, city, state, and federal levels to build out momentum for compensation policies and crafting legislation based on the blueprint set forth in existing laws.

In 2018, Kansas passed legislation providing exonerees with $65,000 for every year of wrongful imprisonment and $25,000 for every year wrongfully served on parole, probation, or the sex offender registry. In addition, the law provides social services, housing and tuition assistance, and counseling. It also provides for full expungement of the conviction.

The law was passed after the personal stories of three wrongfully convicted men were shared with lawmakers. From a strategy standpoint, this is important. The stories of real people like Hassan Bennett, Walter McMillian, Anthony Graves, and Anthony Ray Hinton are important, because in their stories we see our own humanity. We see the possibility that this could happen to anyone.

Of course, these stories can't happen without the misconduct of those who are charged with delivering justice. That's why, when police officers and prosecutors work to break the law rather than uphold it, we must go beyond removing them from their posts. We must prosecute them.

To make this happen, activists must work to put prosecutors in place who will carry out the will of the people. That means actively working against prosecutors who refuse to charge law enforcement officers who engage in criminal misconduct. Activists have already rallied around the issue of police shootings.

In Los Angeles, for example, Black Lives Matter activists made police accountability the top issue in the 2020 race for city district attorney. That message helped them to oust Jackie Lacey, who prosecuted only one police officer during her eight years in office, despite numerous Black people being killed by police in LA.

Activists used the same political pressure campaign to oust two other prosecutors who mishandled high-profile police killings in 2016. Chicago's Cook County state's attorney Anita Alvarez lost her reelection bid after waiting nearly a year to level a first-degree murder charge against former police officer Jason Van Dyke, who shot Laquan McDonald sixteen times, killing him.

Timothy McGinty, the Cuyahoga County prosecuting attorney in

Ohio, lost his bid for reelection after recommending that a grand jury not charge the officers who shot and killed twelve-year-old Tamir Rice.

Activists must use the same strategy to address wrongful convictions. That means targeting and ousting prosecutors who engage in misconduct, and removing those who refuse to prosecute police who engage in misconduct.

Neither prosecutors nor police are immune from prosecution. When they lie, hide evidence, or forcibly coerce witnesses to provide false testimony, they should go to jail, their victims should be compensated, and the lives they destroyed should be made whole, or at least as whole as we can possibly make them.

THE DEMAND

Those who are wrongfully convicted must be compensated, and police officers and prosecutors who commit perjury, tamper with evidence, or coerce witnesses to obtain wrongful convictions must be fired and criminally charged.

4

BREONNA TAYLOR

THE CASE FOR BODY CAMERAS

IT WAS CLOSE TO 1 A.M. ON MARCH 13, 2020, AND BREONNA Taylor and her boyfriend, Kenneth Walker, were asleep in Breonna's apartment at St. Anthony Gardens in Louisville.

Breonna was an emergency room technician at two area hospitals, and like many in the medical field, she'd been working twelve-hour shifts in the first weeks of the coronavirus pandemic. This was her first day off in some time, and Breonna decided to spend it with Kenneth. The couple, both Black, went to dinner at Texas Roadhouse, and afterward, they returned to her apartment to watch the movie *Freedom Writers*. They dozed off during the film, and at 12:40 a.m., they were awakened by someone knocking at the door.

According to numerous media interviews, 911 calls, and a lawsuit Kenneth Walker later filed against the Louisville Metro Police Department, a group of white plainclothes police officers, including police detectives Brett Hankison and Myles Cosgrove and Sgt. Jonathan Mattingly, sought to execute a no-knock warrant at Breonna's apartment. The warrant was connected to an investigation of Jamarcus Glover, Breonna's ex-boyfriend. Police said Glover was a drug dealer, and that Breonna was connected to his drug enterprise. Police had already arrested Glover an hour before in an alleged drug house ten miles away, and the raid on Breonna's apartment was supposed to come off without a hitch. But after police knocked on Breonna's door that night, things didn't go as planned.

Breonna called out to ask who it was, and according to Kenneth, no one answered her question. That's when the two of them got up and started to get dressed, and Kenneth grabbed his gun, because a late-night knock meant that whatever was on the other side of that door might be trouble. He couldn't have known how right he was.

Kenneth said he never heard anyone announce themselves as police, and most of the neighbors who were at home in the apartment complex that night didn't hear them announce themselves either. Police claimed they did announce themselves and that even though they'd specifically sought a no-knock warrant, they first slapped the door with an open hand, and then banged more forcefully. The police account can't be confirmed since the undercover narcotics officers executing the warrant were not wearing body cameras. At the time, departmental policy did not require them to do so, according to a timeline released by the office of Louisville mayor Greg Fischer.

But let me be clear about what I believe took place that night. I'm convinced that the officers knocked on Breonna's door, but they didn't announce themselves as policemen. If they'd done so, Breonna, Kenneth, and their neighbors would've heard them. That's why, when a lieutenant gave the order for the officers to use a battering ram, Breonna and Kenneth were dressed and standing in the hallway outside the bedroom, unsure of who was coming in.

The door burst open in what Kenneth described as an explosion, and in the seconds that followed, Breonna stood with Kenneth as Sergeant Mattingly entered the dark apartment. Mattingly later claimed in police and media interviews that even in the dark, he could see Kenneth standing and aiming a gun directly at him. Kenneth, a licensed gun owner with no criminal record, said he fired a single warning shot at the floor because he believed it was a home invasion. Police shot back, firing a total of thirty-two bullets, and sometime during that exchange, Mattingly was hit in the leg.

As the bullets flew, Kenneth said he grabbed Breonna's hand and pulled her to the floor. He heard her scream, he said, and then she was still. She'd been hit at least five times.

In the midst of the gunfire, neighbors called 911, clearly unaware that police were the ones doing the shooting.

"There was a lot of gunshots just now. . . . They are still shooting," a neighbor named Summer Dickerson said in a 911 call released to the media. "Come on, come on, y'all need to get over here, they're shooting the hell like crazy."[1]

Another neighbor called 911 and said, "They are shooting bad," before adding, "They just unloaded and I heard somebody yell again, 'Reload!'"[2]

In the moments of fear and confusion that followed the gunshots, Kenneth took the same action I did when my mugshot flashed on the television screen and a reporter said I was a wanted fugitive. He took the same action that Anthony Ray Hinton did when he was wrongfully arrested for murder. He reached for the same person George Floyd did when a police officer was choking the life out of him. Kenneth called his mother, and after her panicked son told her that Breonna Taylor had been shot by what he believed to be home invaders, Velicia Walker told her son to hang up and call 911. That's exactly what he did.

"I don't know what's happening," a clearly distraught Kenneth told the 911 dispatcher. "Somebody kicked in the door and shot my girlfriend."[3]

"OK, where are you located?" the dispatcher asked.

"I'm at 3003 Springfield Drive, Apartment 4."

The dispatcher asked Kenneth for Breonna's age. Then she asked him to determine where Breonna had been shot. He answered as best he could, but as the questions continued, he grew more exasperated and distraught.

"I don't know," he said through tears. "She's on the ground right now. I don't know. I don't know."

"Okay," the dispatcher said. "You said she's twenty-six? Is she alert and able to talk to you?"

"No, she's not. Bree! God."

As the dispatcher continued to ask questions, Kenneth repeatedly asked for assistance.

"Help. Oh my God. Yes," he said, when the dispatcher asked him to repeat the apartment number. "Help."

After Kenneth gave his name, the address, and the apartment number again, the dispatcher said, "Okay, can you check and see where she's been shot at?"

"I think the stomach," Kenneth said.

Then, as the dispatcher tried to confirm his previous answers, Kenneth broke down, his words barely audible beneath the sound of his tortured sobs.

He eventually hung up and called Breonna's mother, Tamika Palmer, who tried to call her daughter. When there was no answer, Breonna's mother rushed to get to the apartment complex.

Meanwhile Kenneth Walker was still inside, and dozens of officers were now on the scene, calling for Kenneth to come out. Minutes after the shooting stopped, he did. We know this because the new officers on the scene had body cameras that recorded his surrender.

"Walk back or I'll send this dog!" an officer shouted when Kenneth emerged with his hands raised. "Walk back to me! Keep on walking! Walk now! Walk! Lay your hands on your head, get down on your knees. Get down on your knees. Put your hands behind your head."[4]

Police handcuffed him and Kenneth asked, "What's going on?"

Detective Brett Hankison, one of the three officers who fired into Breonna Taylor's apartment, replied, "You are going to fucking prison, that's what's going on . . . for the rest of your fucking life."[5]

As police questioned him in the parking lot, an officer asked Kenneth, "Who shot at us, you or her?"[6]

"It was her, she was scared," Kenneth said through panic and tears.

In the moments after that, as police escorted the handcuffed Kenneth to a vehicle, he was crying and murmuring a mournful plea. "Please just don't let her be dead," he moaned, his tone low and plaintive. "Please, God, don't let her be dead."[7]

His pleas may have been in vain. According to the *Louisville Courier Journal*, Breonna received no medical help for twenty minutes after she was shot, though the Jefferson County coroner said she likely died within one minute of the bullets piercing her flesh.[8]

Later that day, when Kenneth was questioned by police, he admitted that it was he who fired the single shot when police broke down the door. He was charged with attempted murder in the shooting of Sgt. Jonathan Mattingly.

He wasn't the only one who was traumatized by the night's events. Having rushed to the scene after receiving Kenneth's call, Tamika Palmer arrived at the apartment complex seeking answers about her daughter. Someone told Palmer that she needed to go to the hospital, so she did.

When Breonna's mother reached the hospital, her daughter wasn't there. Thinking she was en route, Tamika Palmer waited for nearly two hours, until finally a hospital staffer told her there was no record of a Breonna Taylor being sent there.

At that, Breonna's mother returned to the apartment complex and questioned several officers, but none of them would give her the answers she was seeking. By the time she was directed to Sgt. Chris Lane, Tamika Palmer told ABC News, she was screaming.

"Why won't you just tell me where Breonna is!" she yelled.[9]

Lane's answer, recorded in audio released to the media, was heartbreaking.

"I'm sorry in advance for you . . . she's in the apartment," Lane said. "Sorry."

At that, Palmer broke down in tears, sobbing because she knew her daughter was dead.

As tragic as that moment was, we know that it occurred because it was recorded on the body cameras of the police officers who arrived after the botched raid.

However, because the first officers on the scene were not wearing body cameras, we can only reconstruct how Breonna died based on Kenneth's recollections, 911 recordings, and the testimony of the officers who killed her. Given that the police version of events is tainted by history, tainted by circumstance, and tainted by the fact that they are the ones who killed Breonna, can we truly trust that their testimony is about telling the truth rather than protecting themselves?

If the officers had worn body cameras, we wouldn't have to ask that question. But they didn't, so there was no video for the world to see, no viral image for the public to debate—only the word of the men who shot and killed Breonna Taylor, and their word clearly wasn't good enough.

That's why the people of Louisville immediately took to the streets in protest. Even though one of the officers, Brett Hankison, was fired fairly quickly for carelessly and repeatedly discharging his weapon that night, it wasn't enough for the people. They believed those officers got away with murder.

The push for police to use body-worn cameras began in Ferguson, Missouri, in 2014, when Officer Darren Wilson killed Michael Brown. Much like Breonna Taylor's death at the hands of Louisville police, the circumstances surrounding Michael Brown's killing were suspicious. Protesters believed the unarmed teen had his hands up in a posture of surrender when

Wilson shot him. However, without body camera footage, Wilson was able to use a familiar narrative to justify killing Michael. He said that he feared for his life. With St. Louis county prosecutor Robert McCulloch helping to bolster that argument before a grand jury, Wilson walked away uncharged and unscathed. The Black community did not fare as well.

Having been scarred by a centuries-long history of abuse at the hands of police, Black Americans were angry after Michael Brown was killed, and they were looking for the first Black president to do something more than utter platitudes.

Among the Obama administration's various responses to Michael's killing, the push for body-worn cameras was unique, because it came with funding. The Obama administration requested $263 million to distribute to police departments to purchase the cameras and to pay for training in using them. The plan was to use $75 million of that federal money to match state funding and pay for fifty thousand body-worn cameras.

Obama also launched a civil rights investigation into Michael Brown's death; convened meetings with police, cabinet members, and civil rights leaders; and announced the creation of the President's Task Force on 21st Century Policing. Its job was to "examine, among other issues, how to promote effective crime reduction while building public trust."[10]

The task force was co-chaired by Philadelphia police commissioner Charles Ramsey and George Mason University professor Laurie Robinson.

In its final report, released in May 2015, body-worn cameras were mentioned nearly two dozen times, and among the task force's fifty-nine recommendations was this: "The U.S. Department of Justice should develop best practices that can be adopted by state legislative bodies to govern the acquisition, use, retention, and dissemination of auditory, visual, and biometric data by law enforcement."

Along with that recommendation, the task force listed an action item: "Law enforcement agencies should review and consider the Bureau of Justice Assistance's (BJA) Body-Worn Camera Toolkit to assist in implementing [body-worn cameras]." That toolkit contains information on funding, technology, implementation, policy recommendations and studies on how the cameras impact policing.

Of course, there are many studies on their use, and the task force included one in its report. The study, "The Effect of Police Body-Worn

Cameras (BWCs) on Use of Force and Citizens' Complaints Against the Police: A Randomized Controlled Trial," was published in the *Journal of Quantitative Criminology* in 2015. Its findings were promising:

> The results of this 12-month study strongly suggest that the use of BWCs by the police can significantly reduce both officer use of force and complaints against officers. The study found that the officers wearing the cameras had 87.5 percent fewer incidents of use of force and 59 percent fewer complaints than the officers not wearing the cameras. One of the important findings of the study was the impact BWCs might have on the self-awareness of officers and citizens alike.
>
> When police officers are acutely aware that their behavior is being monitored (because they turn on the cameras) and when officers tell citizens that the cameras are recording their behavior, everyone behaves better. The results of this study strongly suggest that this increase in self-awareness contributes to more positive outcomes in police-citizen interaction.[11]

After reviewing a variety of research on body-worn cameras, however, one quickly learns that the conclusions can vary based on who conducts the study.

In 2017, an organization called the Lab @ DC announced the results of a study that measured how body-worn cameras affected uses of force and civilian complaints. Like the study cited in the president's task force report, this one used a randomized controlled trial to obtain its results. The study also boasted a large sample size, with more than 2,200 police officers participating.

The study authors assured the public that they prioritized scientific rigor and transparency, creating a detailed write-up of the planned methodology and statistical analyses they would use. They shared that pre-analysis plan before analyzing the data, and their results were stunning.

"We found that body-worn cameras had no statistically significant effects on any of the measured outcomes," the researchers shared in an online version of their study results.[12]

They also shared something else that leaped from the page. The study was designed with the help of the Washington Metro Police Department. For anyone who has thought critically about policing, the assertion that police could design and implement a study of their own behavior is reminiscent of the nonsensical belief that police can objectively investigate themselves.

And yet, that study—designed and implemented by police—was broadly seen as the best research on the efficacy of body-worn cameras.

For example, the conservative-leaning Cato Institute has cited the DC study while offering grudging support for body-worn cameras. However, it has done so while offering commentary featuring headlines like "Hardcore Body Camera Policies Could Do More Harm Than Good," "Body Cameras Worth Deploying Despite Limited Impact," and "Studies Aren't Conclusive—Mandate Them Anyway."[13]

After body-worn cameras recorded images of white, pro-Trump rioters beating Washington Metropolitan Police detective Michael Fanone at the Capitol during the January 6, 2021, insurrection, I'm left to wonder if the Metropolitan Police and their conservative supporters have adjusted their views.

After all, the use of body-worn cameras is about more than changing the behavior of officers or the citizens with whom they interact. Their use is also about collecting evidence, no matter who the culprit or the victim may be. Only that kind of subjective data collection can rebuild trust between police and the communities they patrol—whether they are in Washington, Louisville, or Ferguson.

As Barack Obama said in 2014 when he announced his Task Force on 21st Century Policing, "This is not a problem just of Ferguson, Missouri. This is a national problem."[14]

Obama was right, and long before police killed Breonna Taylor, the 2014 death of Michael Brown sent people scrambling for the numbers to prove Obama's point. That's how America learned that there was no comprehensive database to track all police shootings. The only police shootings tracked by the FBI are those the police deem justifiable. However, local police departments provide those numbers to the FBI on a voluntary basis. They are not required to do so. That has left journalists to try to fill the void.

USA Today analyzed years of data from the FBI's justifiable homicide database and found that during a seven-year period ending in 2012, there were an average of ninety-six incidents a year in which a white police officer killed a Black person.[15]

The Guardian looked at police shootings in 2015 and 2016, and found that in 2016, 24 percent of the shooting victims were Black, though Black Americans make up only 13 percent of the US population. That kind of disproportionality is not uncommon, according to findings by other news organizations.[16]

The *Washington Post* began its own database in 2015 to track police shootings across the country. The *Post* found that as of December 2020, 24 percent of those killed by police in the last five years were Black.[17]

In short, Michael Brown was not unique. That makes it all the more troubling that six years after the Obama administration put a task force in place and funded the use of body-worn cameras, Breonna Taylor was killed in her own apartment by police who were not wearing them.

The adoption of body-worn cameras was not supposed to be this difficult, but just as the system of policing fights to control the narrative around individual shootings, the system fights to control what the public sees.

That's why, even when police video of a controversial incident is available, it is sometimes held back from public view for weeks or months at a time. That must change.

But there must also be a concerted effort to make body-worn cameras mandatory for police officers. In cases like Breonna Taylor's, where so many things went wrong, the images from such cameras could have served as the evidence needed to corroborate the truth.

However, the absence of body cameras wasn't the only way the criminal justice system failed Breonna. The events that led to her death began long before police arrived.

Born in Grand Rapids, Michigan, in 1993, Breonna Taylor, like most kids, was trying to find her way as a middle schooler. She found a friend in Alena Battle, who recalled Breonna as someone who was fun to be around.

Reached by NBC News in the months after her friend died, Alena, who was a year younger than Breonna, said the two of them were kindred spirits who bonded over their love of board games and their love for each other.

Their families lived in the same townhouse development in Grand Rapids, but even after Breonna and her family moved to Kentucky in 2008, her friendship with Alena remained strong. They were so close that when Alena gave birth to her son, Tamaj, she asked Breonna to be his godmother, knowing that if Tamaj ever needed someone, Breonna would be there for him.

Breonna's younger sister Ju'Niyah described Breonna the same way—as a good person who simply did right by others. Ju'Niyah, who lived with Breonna but was not at home on the night of the shooting, told NBC News that Breonna's work in the medical field fit her personality.

She loved helping people, and until 2016, she was an emergency medical technician for Louisville Metro Emergency Medical Services, working fifteen-hour shifts. Her sister Ju'Niyah said the long hours would leave Breonna so drained that Breonna would come home, eat a bowl of Fruity Pebbles, and fall asleep.

Breonna went on to work as a PRN—or pro re nata—at Norton Hospital. That means she filled in on an as-needed basis as a medical worker. She also worked as an ER technician at Jewish Hospital. Along the way, her relationships continued to play a key role in her life. She played cards with her aunts, who also work in the healthcare field. She remained close with her mother, who works as a dialysis technician.

But it was her relationship with Jamarcus Glover that interested police. Glover, who had prior drug convictions, was a former boyfriend of Breonna's. Police began surveilling Glover's activities in January 2020, alleging that he was selling drugs in a high-crime area on Elliot Avenue in Louisville. Police alleged that Glover retrieved a package from Breonna's apartment, and during one of Glover's stints in jail, they recorded several calls he made to Breonna.

Police requested multiple warrants in connection with their investigation of Glover. One of them, requested by Louisville police detective Joshua Jaynes, was a no-knock search warrant for Breonna's apartment, because police believed Breonna was holding drugs and money for Glover.

Jaynes asked a judge to approve the warrant, claiming that a postal inspector verified that Glover was receiving packages at Breonna's apartment. Here, in part, is what Jaynes wrote in an affidavit to justify the issuance of a no-knock warrant:

> On 1/16/2020, during the afternoon hours, Affiant witnessed Jamarcus Glover operating the listed red 2017 Dodge Charger. Mr. J. Glover pulled up and parked in front of (redacted). Affiant then observed Mr. J. Glover walk directly into apartment #4. After a short period of time, Mr. J. Glover was seen exiting the apartment with a suspected USPS package in his right hand. Mr. Glover then got into the red 2017 Dodge Charger and drove straight to (redacted) which is a known drug house.

> Affiant verified through a US Postal Inspector that Jamarcus Glover has been receiving packages at (redacted). Affiant knows through training and experience that it is not uncommon for drug traffickers to receive mail packages at different locations to avoid detection from law enforcement. Affiant believes through training and experience, that Mr. J. Glover may be keeping narcotics and/or proceeds from the sale of narcotics at (redacted) for safe keeping.[18]

The problem with Jaynes's statement is this: Louisville postal inspector Tony Gooden told a local news outlet that his office never received a request from the Louisville Metro Police Department to investigate whether Breonna's apartment was receiving suspicious mail.

While Gooden went on to say that he received a request from another law enforcement agency regarding Breonna's apartment, his office conducted an investigation and found that she was not receiving any suspicious mail.

Still, Jaynes wrote in his affidavit that a US postal inspector verified that Glover received packages at Breonna's apartment and added that the no-knock warrant was requested "due to the nature of how these drug traffickers operate. These drug traffickers have a history of attempting to destroy evidence, have cameras on the location that compromise Detectives once an approach to the dwelling is made, and have a history of fleeing from law enforcement."[19]

So, Breonna, who had no criminal record, was lumped in as a drug trafficker in Jaynes's affidavit, and based on that document, the no-knock warrant was approved by Jefferson County judge Mary Shaw.

And yet, after obtaining that no-knock warrant to deal with "these drug traffickers" who "have a history of fleeing from law enforcement," the police officers who carried out the raid claimed they knocked on Breonna's door more than once, repeatedly announced that they were police officers, and only then forced the door open with a battering ram.

Even if, as the police later said, they believed Breonna was home alone and that her apartment was a soft target, why go to the trouble of getting a no-knock warrant if their intention was to knock and announce themselves?

The police version of the events surrounding the use of the no-knock warrant defies reason, and a number of governmental actions in the wake of Breonna's death make it clear that prosecutors and politicians understood that.

First, there was the fate of Kenneth Walker, the licensed gun owner who was with Breonna and fired a single shot when police burst into the apartment. Kenneth maintained throughout the ordeal that he believed the police were intruders. Initially, Kenneth was charged with attempted murder for allegedly shooting Sgt. Jonathan Mattingly, but the charges against him were dropped and he was released. Kenneth later filed suit against the Louisville Metro Police Department.

In addition, Louisville's local government clearly saw the Breonna Taylor case as a textbook example of why no-knock warrants should never be used.

Less than three months after police killed Breonna in her apartment while executing that no-knock warrant, Louisville Metro Council unanimously passed a bill to ban their use, and Louisville mayor Greg Fischer signed the legislation. They call it Breonna's Law, and here is what it says:

> No Louisville Metro Police Department (LMPD) police officer, Louisville Metro Department of Corrections (LMDC) officer, or any other Metro law enforcement or public safety official shall seek, execute, or participate in the execution of a no-knock warrant at any location within the boundaries of Jefferson County.[20]

That law should be replicated in every jurisdiction, but banning no-knock warrants is not enough. Just as it did in the Michael Brown case, the secretive and politically flawed grand jury system helped deny justice in Breonna's killing.

Kentucky attorney general Daniel Cameron, a Black conservative Republican, impaneled the grand jury that considered evidence in Breonna's death. Like St. Louis County's Robert McCulloch in the Michael Brown case, Cameron was a pro-police prosecutor who'd run for office while promising to consistently support police.

Because grand jury investigations are run completely by prosecutors, the evidence they present and the recommendations they make to grand jurors generally shape the outcome. Things were no different in Breonna's case.

Cameron presented the grand jurors with evidence and recommended that they indict one of the officers, Brett Hankison, on three charges of first-degree wanton endangerment. Cameron's recommendation was not based on the fact that police officers killed Breonna. Rather, it was predicated on the fact that some of the bullets police fired endangered three people in a neighboring apartment.

Cameron, who never gave the grand jury the option to pursue murder charges in connection with Breonna's death, said at a press conference that "the grand jury agreed" that the officers were justified in returning fire after they were shot at by Breonna's boyfriend, Kenneth Walker. He also claimed at the press conference that he "walked the grand jury through every homicide offense."[21]

After Cameron made those statements, one of the grand jurors filed suit in order to speak out about the normally secret proceedings, and was cleared by a judge to do so.

In a statement, the anonymous juror said the panel "didn't agree that certain actions were justified," and grand jurors "did not have homicide charges explained to them."

The statement also said, "The grand jury never heard anything about those laws. Self-defense or justification was never explained either."

Cameron tried to defend his actions as public outrage grew, speaking to a local ABC station in Bowling Green, Kentucky. "It was not our judgment that there should be other charges that the grand jury should be advised of," Cameron said in the interview.[22]

"The grand jury can, you know, as an independent body, bring up other questions or other issues," he added. "I fully take responsibility for the recommendation that we made. Based on the facts, that was the appropriate recommendation to make."

Cameron's mishandling of this case is yet another reason why the grand jury system must be dismantled. Justice for Black people should never be ruled on in secret proceedings created by racist systems. Cameron, as a Black man, illustrates that racism can be carried out by Black people. Within the criminal justice system, it was Cameron's job to protect the police officers, even if that meant devaluing the life of an innocent Black woman. He did that job all too well, but his assertion that "the facts" led him to make an "appropriate recommendation" illustrates the bigger problem. We don't know all the facts, because the officers who burst into Breonna's apartment were not wearing body cameras.

We must never again allow that to happen. Not only should officers who unjustly kill Black people be charged with homicide. They must also face criminal consequences for seeking to destroy or limit evidence through the misuse of body cameras.

The strategy for implementing this demand centers on protest, political activism, and replication of current legislation.

According to the National Conference of State Legislatures, California, Nevada, South Carolina, Florida, and Connecticut have enacted laws that require some officers to use body-worn cameras. In order to make their use required by all officers, the effort must be state by state, and it must be based on a legislative blueprint. To find it, we must look to Tennessee.

In February 2019, Tennessee state representative G. A. Hardaway and state senator Sara Kyle introduced bills that would make it a Class E felony for police officers to turn off their body-worn cameras in an effort to obstruct justice.

The legislation sought to strengthen a law that allows prosecutors to file charges against police officers who turn off their body-worn cameras for tampering with evidence.

Under Hardaway and Kyle's legislation, the punishment is specific. As Hardaway told CNN, the bill makes it clear that "failure of the device to capture certain evidence due to intentional acts on behalf of police officers is unacceptable."[23]

As a Class E felony, a violation of the law would be punishable by one to two years in prison.

Advocating for such legislation requires protest. The target of such demonstrations are not police, but elected officials. As representatives of the communities most impacted by police violence, they are our employees. Therefore, the community must demand that their representatives not only propose this legislation but shepherd it through the process of passage. Failure to do so must result in the targeted representative being removed and replaced.

Given the rage, trauma, and pain that Breonna's unjust killing created in the Black community, passing such legislation is the least we can do.

THE DEMAND

Officers who disable body cameras or fail to wear them during deadly encounters must be criminally charged. They must face discipline, up to and including firing, for disabling cameras during any encounter. Police departments must also be made to share footage of any police activity with the public upon request. Both the cameras and the footage are taxpayer-funded property and should be treated as such. In addition, the use of no-knock warrants must be banned in every jurisdiction.

5

ERIC GARNER

THE CASE FOR PUBLIC RECORDS

IN THE EARLY AFTERNOON OF JULY 17, 2014, NEW YORK Police lieutenant Christopher Bannon was driving to a meeting when he spotted a group of men at Bay Street and Victory Boulevard on Staten Island. They appeared to be selling individual cigarettes—commonly known as loosies. Such activity was not unusual there.

However, the community was starting to gentrify, and authorities in New York were focusing on quality-of-life issues—a strategy often referred to as "broken windows" policing. Bannon, who is white, didn't have time to stop himself, so he called back to the 120th precinct and told the desk sergeant to send officers to clear the corner. The police viewed the men selling loosies along Bay Street as negative "conditions" that needed to be dealt with. Eric Garner was one of those men.

Standing six feet two and weighing over 350 pounds, Eric was hard to miss, and the police rarely did. The Black father of six had already been arrested or harassed numerous times for selling loosies on Staten Island. In his most recent encounter, which occurred earlier that month, Eric was approached by police and flailed his arms and complained of harassment until they let him go with a warning. This time would be different, though. With their commanders pressuring them to do something about the corner, the officers couldn't come back empty-handed.

As the lieutenant's edict made its way to the two officers who would eventually arrive on Bay Street, Eric went about his day, oblivious to what was coming.

After eating lunch with his friend Ramsey Orta, who is Latino and twenty years younger than Eric, he saw two men get into a heated argument. A witness named Taisha Allen told the *New York Times* that one of the men was a father. The other was a man who was known on the block as Twin. The father accused Twin of saying something disrespectful to his daughter. Then he punched Twin in the face, prompting Eric Garner to jump between them and hold them apart.

"You can't keep doing this," Eric said, according to Allen's recollection. "There are kids out here."[1]

The role of peacemaker was a familiar one for Eric, who was described by friends as a gentle giant. His interest in stopping fights was not entirely altruistic, though. Eric, a devoted husband and father, supported his family by selling loose, untaxed cigarettes on Bay Street. Fights attracted police, and police were bad for business.

In fact, the denizens of Bay Street thought the two white plainclothes officers who showed up a few minutes later were there about the fight. However, when the officers got out of the car after circling the block twice, they didn't try to find the fighters. They instead made a beeline for the big man in the gray T-shirt and cargo shorts—the man who had made the fighters move on.

Eric immediately recognized one of the cops. His name was John D'Amico, and he was the 120th precinct's "quality of life coordinator." D'Amico had stopped Eric two weeks earlier for allegedly selling loose cigarettes and let him go with a warning. The other officer, Daniel Pantaleo, normally worked in a unit that handled violent street crime. Both were veterans of the force—D'Amico had approximately four years of experience, and Pantaleo had about eight.

When they approached Eric, there was some back-and-forth between Eric and the officers before Ramsey Orta raised his phone and started filming. Taisha Allen, who is Black, also recorded parts of the encounter and its aftermath. Police transcripts compiled from several videos and reviewed by the *New York Times* say Eric was exasperated when D'Amico approached him.

"What are you talking about?" Eric asked D'Amico. "I didn't do anything. I didn't sell anything. I didn't sell nothing. I didn't do shit. . . . Minding my business, a fight breaks out. I stopped it. . . . The people that's fighting, you just let them walk away? Are you serious?"[2]

As Ramsey Orta continued to film the interaction, D'Amico told Orta, whose bike was nearby, to "take a ride down the block."

"I live here," Orta said.

Then, as a Black woman stepped into the frame to ask for Officer D'Amico's name, which he gave her, Eric continued to protest his innocence.

"I didn't do nothing," Eric said. "What did I do?"[3]

D'Amico asked Eric for identification, and Eric told him he didn't have it. Then, when D'Amico said they were going to take him in, Eric questioned him again.

"Take me back for what?" he said. "I didn't sell anything. I did nothing. We sitting here the whole time, minding our business."

D'Amico told Eric that he saw him sell cigarettes.

Eric asked, "Who did I sell a cigarette to? To who?"[4]

D'Amico pointed up the street and referenced someone wearing a red shirt. Eric Garner grew more upset. Ramsey Orta complained loudly that Eric was being harassed for breaking up a fight. Observers gathered around them, and Eric became more agitated.

The exchange continued for a few seconds more, and D'Amico gave an ultimatum. "We can do this the easy way or the hard way," he said.

"Easy way or the hard way for what?" Eric said. "Every time you see me you want to mess with me. I'm tired of it. This stops today. No. What you bothering me for? Everybody standing here they'll tell you I didn't do nothing. I did not sell nothing."

D'Amico asked Eric a question that was difficult to hear in the video, but Eric's answer was clear.

"Because every time you see me, you want to harass me," he said. "You want to stop me talkin' about I'm selling cigarettes. I'm minding my business, officer. I'm minding my business. Please just leave me alone. I told you the last time, please just leave me alone."

Pantaleo, who had called for backup during the exchange, positioned himself behind Eric Garner and told him to put his hands behind his back.

"Please, please don't touch me," Eric said. "Do not touch me."

That's when Pantaleo put one of his arms under Eric's arm and the other around his neck. As Pantaleo employed the chokehold, the two men tumbled against the glass window of a beauty supply store. Then, as Pantaleo held on, they fell to the ground with Pantaleo's arm still fastened tightly around Eric Garner's neck.

Three other officers, including D'Amico, moved in to hold Eric down as Pantaleo pressed Eric's head against the pavement.

"I can't breathe. I can't breathe. I can't breathe. I can't breathe. I can't breathe. I can't breathe. I can't breathe. I can't breathe," Eric said, begging for air as the officers violently restrained him.

While Eric struggled for his next breath, a Black uniformed patrol sergeant named Kizzy Adonis stepped into the frame of Orta's video. Two witnesses, including beauty store manager Rodney Lee, told the *New York Times* that Sergeant Adonis told the officers to "let up" on Eric, since he'd already been subdued.[5]

The officers did not appear to obey that order, and as the struggle ended with Eric Garner lying motionless on the ground, the sergeant who'd sent the officers to Bay Street showed up at the scene.

"What's going on?" precinct sergeant Dhanan Saminath asked Pantaleo, according to the *Washington Post*. "How did this happen?"[6]

After Pantaleo offered his version of events, Saminath, who is Asian, told the officers to search the dying man. They did so, and allegedly found four packs of Newports in the pockets of Eric's cargo shorts. Sergeant Saminath also asked if an ambulance had been called. He was told that it was on the way.

When the ambulance arrived from Richmond University Medical Center at 3:36 p.m., Emergency Medical Technician Nicole Palmieri, who is white, checked for a pulse.

"Sir. It's EMS," Palmieri said to Eric. "C'mon. We're here to help, all right. We're here to help you. We're getting the stretcher. All right?"[7]

Eric was unresponsive, but Palmieri did not render any assistance to him—a move that befuddled bystanders who repeatedly asked why no one was trying to resuscitate Eric.

While Palmieri checked for a pulse, another EMT, Stephanie Greenberg, walked back to the ambulance for the stretcher. An EMT trainee followed Greenberg, walking away from Eric with the oxygen equipment he needed.

As bystanders continued to ask why no one was trying to render medical aid, they were told by a police officer that Eric was breathing. Of the five medical workers who responded to the scene, none of them gave him oxygen as he lay on the ground.

According to hospital records, by the time they got Eric onto the stretcher, he went into cardiac arrest. Sergeant Saminath told D'Amico and Pantaleo to escort the ambulance to the hospital. Then, at 4:11 p.m., Saminath sent a text message to Lt. Chris Bannon, whose earlier call to the precinct had set the day's events in motion.

"Danny and Justin went to collar Eric Garner and he resisted," Saminath wrote in the text message. "When they took him down he went into cardiac arrest and is unconscious. Might be DOA."

"For the smokes?" Bannon replied.

"Yeah, they observed him selling," Saminath answered, adding that an ambulance had been called. "Danny tried to grab him and they both fell down. He's most likely DOA. . . . He has no pulse."[8]

Christopher Bannon wrote a four-word response while Eric Garner lay dying as the result of one of his officer's actions.

"Not a big deal," Bannon wrote via text message.

By 4:15, emergency room doctors could not detect Eric's pulse, and at 4:34, they declared him dead.[9]

The fight for justice in the death of Eric Garner seemed to have everything necessary to succeed. There was the viral video, which clearly showed that Officer Daniel Pantaleo had employed a chokehold—a move banned by the New York Police Department (NYPD) since the 1990s. There was police chief William Bratton admitting that Pantaleo appeared to use a chokehold. There were Eric Garner's last words, "I can't breathe," which served as a potent rallying cry. There were protesters of every stripe who were angered by what they saw. But in spite of all that, the fight for justice in Eric Garner's death was no match for the system set up to fight against it.

Officer Daniel Pantaleo, whose chokehold immediately became the focus of the fight, was shielded by a police department and a police union. Both quickly closed ranks to protect him.

Just hours after Eric died, a report known as a 49 was prepared for police commanders. That five-page internal report made no mention of the chokehold. In fact, it made no mention of any officer making contact with Eric's neck.

The report also quoted a witness named Taisha Allen as saying that "the two officers each took Mr. Garner by the arms and put him on the ground."[10]

Taisha Allen told the *New York Times* that the statement the police claimed she made was inaccurate. Video of the incident backed her claim and made it plain that Pantaleo had indeed used a chokehold to bring down Eric Garner.

It was the video, in fact, that aided in medical examiner Floriana Persechino's determination of the cause of death. Persechino, who at the time was a twenty-year veteran of the medical examiner's office, watched the footage of Eric's last moments, and after performing her autopsy, determined "compression of the neck, chokehold,"[11] as the cause of death. She listed chest compression, asthma, and hypertension as contributing factors.

She determined that the manner of death was homicide.

But even as the medical examiner made it clear that Eric Garner's life was taken on that fateful day in Staten Island, the criminal justice system was lining up to protect the man who was responsible for that violent act.

Police officers were posted outside Pantaleo's home to provide physical protection, and he was placed on desk duty, where he continued to receive a paycheck and benefits during a yearslong investigation of the incident. There was also protection at the state level through Section 50-a of the New York State Civil Rights Law, which effectively prevented the public from seeing Pantaleo's disciplinary records for years.

Initially adopted in 1976, the law allowed law enforcement officers to refuse disclosure of "personnel records used to evaluate performance toward continued employment or promotion."[12] It was meant to keep defense lawyers from using those records in cross-examination of police witnesses during criminal prosecutions, but over the years it was expanded by the courts to allow police departments to hide virtually any record containing any information that could be used to evaluate the performance of a police officer.

Then there were the police unions. Politically powerful advocates that often help shield officers from accountability, those unions and their leaders spoke forcefully against the obvious—that Pantaleo had employed a chokehold in the minutes leading up to Eric Garner's death.

The Police Benevolent Association (PBA), the union representing Pantaleo, was front and center in that effort. PBA president Patrick Lynch claimed that Pantaleo did not use a chokehold, even though millions of people saw the officer do so in the video. A little more than two weeks after Eric's death, shortly before a special session of New York's Civilian

Complaint Review Board to examine the use of police chokeholds, Lynch repeated his assertion.

"It was not a chokehold," Lynch said, as other police union leaders representing officers and sergeants stood around him, along with lawyers representing Officer Pantaleo. "It was bringing a person to the ground the way we're trained to do to place him under arrest. You put your arm on them and bring them down."[13]

Edward Mullins, the head of the sergeants' police union, called on his members to supervise every arrest, a move that would amount to a work slowdown. He added that chief medical examiner Floriana Persechino's use of the word "chokehold" in her final autopsy report was political rather than factual.

Mullins's decision to accuse the chief medical examiner of playing politics appeared to be hyperbole. But there were others whose political ambitions were influenced by their handling of Eric Garner's death.

New York mayor Bill de Blasio, who was elected with the help of the city's Black and brown communities after promising to reform racist stop-and-frisk policies, tried to play both sides. It didn't work. De Blasio, who is married to a Black woman and has biracial children, acknowledged instances of excessive force by police and encouraged people to protest peacefully. But in the eyes of activists, he didn't do enough to seek justice for Eric Garner or to punish the officer who killed him. It was a criticism that would hound him for years.

The law enforcement community wasn't pleased with de Blasio either. They saw him as an anti-police mayor who was too closely linked to activists like Al Sharpton. In fact, police were so incensed over what they saw as de Blasio's anti-police rhetoric that when two New York policemen were shot and killed four months after Eric's death, cops turned their backs on de Blasio when he visited the mortally wounded officers at a Brooklyn hospital.

However, there were others whose political ambitions were firmly attached to their handling of the Eric Garner case. Among them was Staten Island district attorney Dan Donovan.

The Staten Island DA was no stranger to working closely with police unions. In 2011, Donovan was endorsed for a third term as district attorney by the Police Benevolent Association—the same union that represented Officer Pantaleo. PAB president Patrick Lynch—the man who later claimed that Pantaleo did not use a chokehold in the death of Eric Garner—called Donovan their "partner" who had "earned" their endorsement.[14]

In 2014, after Eric was killed, Donovan continued to act as a partner to the police, rather than a seeker of justice. Like St. Louis County prosecutor Robert McCulloch in the Michael Brown case, and Kentucky attorney general Daniel Cameron in the Breonna Taylor case, Donovan used the secret and easily manipulated grand jury process to determine whether charges would be filed against Officer Pantaleo in the death of Eric Garner.

The secrecy of grand jury proceedings, like other mechanisms employed in the Eric Garner case, served to protect Pantaleo, but it did not bring about justice for Eric Garner.

Taisha Allen, the witness who filmed the inadequate response of emergency medical workers, told the grand jury that she saw Pantaleo put Eric Garner in a chokehold. According to the *New York Times*, Rodney Lee, the beauty store manager, told grand jurors about police sergeant Kizzy Adonis ordering Pantaleo and other officers to ease up on Eric—an order the officers ignored. Lee also told the *Times* that grand jurors seemed uninterested in his testimony. In the end, neither eyewitness testimony nor multiple videos swayed the grand jurors, but Pantaleo apparently did.

In a summary of his grand jury testimony provided to various media outlets by police union lawyer Stuart London, Pantaleo told grand jurors that he was trying a takedown move and only grabbed Eric's neck to keep them both from crashing through the glass storefront of the beauty supply store where the confrontation took place. He also told grand jurors that he meant Eric Garner no harm.

Ultimately, District Attorney Dan Donovan, the prosecutor who controlled the proceedings, presented evidence that failed to result in an indictment of Officer Pantaleo. He bristled at that description of his actions, however.

"I always try to correct people when they say, 'You failed to get an indictment,'" Donovan told the Associated Press. "That means that our goal should have been to get one. And our goal is to present fair and impartial evidence to 23 members of our community."[15]

However, it was impossible to gauge what Donovan's true goal was since he released so little information about the grand jury proceedings, and to be clear, it didn't have to be that way. In New York, district attorneys or prosecutors are the only ones who can request the release of grand jury information. Donovan submitted a request to release only the number of witnesses and the type of evidence they reviewed.

That meant no one could see transcripts of witness testimony, surveillance video, or autopsy reports. It meant that the grand jury in the Eric Garner case operated largely in the shadows, away from public scrutiny.

By way of comparison, even Robert McCulloch, the St. Louis County prosecutor who was so closely linked to police that he was asked to recuse himself from the Michael Brown case later that year, publicly released all available grand jury evidence.

Donovan did just the opposite. And, while he was widely criticized nationally, many residents of Staten Island, a conservative borough heavily populated by police officers and firefighters, did not see transparency as a priority in the Eric Garner case. For Donovan, who had his sights set on being elected to higher office, indicting a police officer in the on-duty killing of a Black man would have been a political risk. Failing to indict meant succeeding politically.

In May 2015, just months after convening the grand jury that failed to indict Pantaleo, and fighting to keep the testimony and other evidence secret, Donovan was elected to Congress to represent Staten Island and parts of Brooklyn. He was endorsed by two powerful police unions—the Captains Endowment Association and the Lieutenants Benevolent Association.

In another example of the broken systems that are consistently activated in cases like Eric Garner's, the police department launched an internal investigation, but this time, there was a twist. The department announced that their findings would be delayed until a civil rights inquiry by the US attorney for the Eastern District of New York was completed.

That federal investigation was marred by politics from the very beginning. While prosecutors and FBI officials in New York opposed bringing charges because they didn't think they could win a conviction, prosecutors with the Justice Department's Civil Rights Division in Washington argued there was clear evidence to bring charges.

Loretta Lynch, who oversaw the beginning of the investigation as the US attorney for the Eastern District of New York and later became attorney general, spent months considering how to proceed. However, the case languished for years, even as the deaths of other Black people at the hands of police drove public outcry and angry protests.

Michael Brown was killed in Ferguson, Missouri. Laquan McDonald was killed in Chicago. Tamir Rice was killed in Cleveland. Walter Scott was killed in South Carolina. Freddie Gray was killed in Baltimore, and in Texas, Sandra Bland died in police custody under questionable circumstances. And still, in spite of all this, there was no resolution in the federal civil rights case over the death of Eric Garner.

Meanwhile, New York City reached a $5.9 million civil settlement with Eric's family to settle their wrongful death claim, and the Richmond University Medical Center agreed to pay $1 million to the family over the botched response by ambulance personnel.

But even as others paid for the actions of Pantaleo, he had thus far paid no significant price himself. Throughout the various investigations, Pantaleo continued to be paid as a New York police officer, his disciplinary records continued to be hidden from the public, grand jury testimony in the case remained sealed, and justice for Eric's family remained elusive.

It wasn't until 2019, nearly five years after Eric was killed on a street corner for selling loose cigarettes, that his family received some semblance of a day in court. Even then, the proceedings took place under ground rules set by the police department—the same people who killed Eric Garner.

The hearing happened in a fourth-floor room at New York police headquarters. There, Stuart London, a lawyer provided by the police union to defend Pantaleo, faced off against Jonathan Fogel, a prosecutor with the Civilian Complaint Review Board. The two would question and cross-examine a slew of witnesses during an internal administrative process to decide whether Pantaleo should be fired for using the chokehold that helped kill Eric Garner.

The hearing, which included more than twenty hours of testimony from fourteen witnesses, painted a stark picture of the inner workings of a system designed to protect its own.[16]

For instance, the yearslong delay before the hearing took place worked in Pantaleo's favor. Because so much time had passed since Eric was killed, police department rules mandated that prosecutors had to go beyond simply proving that Pantaleo used a chokehold—which the video clearly showed that he did. Prosecutors also had to prove that Pantaleo's use of the chokehold rose to the level of criminal conduct.

Bear in mind that the police department delayed the hearing, claiming that they wanted to wait for the outcome of the federal investigation. Given that the federal investigation still had not concluded, one could reasonably question whether the department waited to make it harder to prove a case against Pantaleo.

The systemic racism baked into the hearing played out in those rules, and the racial separation played out in that room.

Each day during the hearings, Pantaleo's family and a largely white throng of police union officials sat behind the defense table. Eric's family was on the other side, with an almost all Black cast of politicians and activists sitting behind the prosecutors.

The testimony varied, with prosecutors seeking to prove what the rest of the world had already plainly seen—that Daniel Pantaleo's chokehold led to the death of Eric Garner.

Prosecutors called NYPD inspector Richard Dee to the stand. A thirty-year police veteran, he was a high-ranking commander in the department's recruit training unit.

Dee reviewed the video frame by frame, concluding that there was no doubt about the maneuver executed by Pantaleo. "It meets the definition of a chokehold," Dee testified. "I'm not saying he intentionally did that. But that's where his arms are."

Internal Affairs investigators also called Pantaleo's maneuver a chokehold. So did medical examiner Floriana Persechino, who testified that she viewed the video of Eric's death and saw "air hunger"—Eric's body reacting to a craving for oxygen. She said Pantaleo's chokehold began a "lethal cascade," triggering an asthma attack that led to cardiac arrest.[17]

The defense, meanwhile, sought to deny that Pantaleo had used a chokehold at all. Police union attorney Stuart London claimed that Pantaleo used what is known as a "seat belt" hold and takedown, which is taught at the police academy. He blamed Eric for his own death, repeatedly saying that he died because of his poor health and his decision to resist arrest.

"He died from being morbidly obese," London said during the hearing. "He was a ticking time bomb that resisted arrest. If he was put in a bear hug, it would have been the same outcome."

In some ways, Stuart London was right. The situation was the result of a ticking time bomb. Except the ticking time bomb was not Eric Garner. The time bomb was systemic racism.

It ticks when authorities define a Black man selling untaxed cigarettes as a "condition" to be handled. It ticks when systems intersect to protect those who wrongly take Black lives. It ticks when those who handle the levers of power are rewarded with higher office for hiding information from the public. It ticks when a police officer continues to collect a taxpayer-funded salary and benefits for years after killing an unarmed man on a street corner.

Eric, who worked for the city of New York as a horticulturalist before quitting for health reasons, had value. As a father of six who was fiercely devoted to his family, he had value. As a husband who had been with his wife for twenty years, he had value. As a foodie who could eat a whole pizza like a taco, as a caretaker who gave children dollar bills to buy ice cream, as a street debater who liked a good argument, as a thinker who played chess and checkers in Tompkinsville Park, as a human being who had every right to live, Eric Garner had value.

But after he was killed due to the actions of a police officer, Eric Garner's life was reduced to the thirty times he'd been arrested, mostly for selling loose untaxed cigarettes. His life was reduced to his size, his health, his attitude, and his Blackness. And in a last cynical attempt to protect the man whose chokehold led to Eric's death, the system that helped kill him laid the blame at Eric's feet.

Perhaps, if there were no video, no protests, and no outrage, that would have been enough to make it all go away. But Eric's videotaped death sparked international outrage, and no matter how many times it was denied, the world saw how Eric died. Given all that was done to shield Daniel Pantaleo from accountability, it was still a shock when even a tiny measure of punishment was handed down.

In August 2019, deputy police commissioner Rosemarie Maldonado, who acted as administrative judge in Pantaleo's disciplinary hearing, found Pantaleo guilty of "reckless assault" when he used a banned chokehold on Eric. She found the officer not guilty of "intentional strangulation" and recommended that he be fired.

Shortly after, police commissioner James O'Neill fired Pantaleo and stripped him of his pension.

In doing so, O'Neill voiced sympathy not only for Eric Garner's family but also for Pantaleo. The commissioner claimed that he might have made the same fatal mistakes if he had been in Pantaleo's place.

"Every time I watched the video, I say to myself, as probably all of you do, to Mr. Garner: 'Don't do it. Comply,'" O'Neill said. "To Officer Pantaleo: 'Don't do it.' I said that about the decisions made by both Officer Pantaleo and Mr. Garner."[18]

That sort of doublespeak, which seeks to place the perpetrator in the role of victim and lays blame on the victim, is part and parcel of the systemic racism that undergirds policing in the United States. More than that, O'Neill attempted to paint the conditions of the neighborhood as something that lent context to Pantaleo's chokehold—as if a neighborhood where drug dealers worked the edges of the park while men like Eric sold loose cigarettes made Pantaleo's actions more palatable.

"Neighborhood residents purposely avoided the area in and directly around Tompkinsville Park," O'Neill said. "Drug dealers worked the edges of the park, and across the street, selling narcotics. A handful of men regularly sold loose cigarettes made cheaper by the fact that New York State taxes had not been paid on them. A liquor store nearby sold alcohol to people who would drink that alcohol in the park—people who would sometimes use drugs, urinate and pass out on benches there."

Again, this kind of demonization of the community does not nullify or justify Pantaleo's actions. In fact, if drug dealing and public urination was a problem there, wasn't that the purview of the police department? Should they have made the park safe for neighborhood residents? And shouldn't they have been able to do so without killing Eric Garner?

Policing is hard work, O'Neill said, adding that it sometimes involves split-second, life-and-death choices.

"The unintended consequence of Mr. Garner's death must have a consequence of its own," O'Neill said. "It is clear that Daniel Pantaleo can no longer effectively serve as a New York City police officer."

With that, Pantaleo was fired, and while he never faced criminal charges for employing the chokehold that resulted in Eric Garner's death, there is another penalty that must be enforced. Pantaleo should never again be allowed to work as a police officer.

To be clear, Pantaleo and many others in law enforcement do not share that sentiment. In fact, Pantaleo sued to get his job back shortly after he was dismissed from the police department. He claimed that his firing was arbitrary and capricious.

As bizarre as it might seem that Pantaleo could somehow return to his job at the NYPD or find employment in another police department, there is ample chance that he could do just that.

In a 2020 study published in the *Yale Law Journal*, researchers tracked police officers in Florida over a thirty-year period. They found that in any given year, 3 percent of current full-time officers had previously been fired by other law enforcement agencies in the state. The findings got more disturbing from there.

The researchers found that police officers who are fired in Florida are typically rehired by another agency in three years or less. When they are rehired, they tend to move to smaller law enforcement agencies with fewer resources and larger communities of color. Not surprisingly, the study found that these officers get fired about twice as often as other officers and are more likely to receive "moral character violations" for things like physical and sexual misconduct.

That's not just the reality in Florida. It happens all over the country with deadly consequences. That's especially true in communities of color, where police abuse is statistically more likely to occur.

Darren Wilson was among those fired when the town of Jennings, Missouri, disbanded its police department in 2011 amid claims that the overwhelmingly white police force was engaged in racist treatment of Black citizens. Wilson applied for a job in nearby Ferguson, where he killed unarmed black teen Michael Brown in an infamous 2014 shooting that spurred national protests.

Timothy Loehmann was a patrolman in training in Independence, Ohio, when a firearms instructor said Loehmann was "distracted" and "weepy" during firearms training. Deputy Chief Jim Polak of the Independence Police Department recommended terminating Loehmann, who resigned before he could be fired. But by 2014, Loehmann was a rookie patrolman in the Cleveland police department when he shot and killed twelve-year-old Tamir Rice, a Black child who was playing with a toy gun at the time.

But there are many lesser-known instances of police officers being fired for misconduct or even criminal activity, only to get a job with another law enforcement agency.

Kevin Schnell was a police officer in Kansas City in 2006 when he and Officer Melody Spencer stopped Sofia Salva, a Black woman who was suspected of having fake temporary tags on the vehicle she was driving. During the stop, the officers discovered that Salva had outstanding warrants, and ignored her repeated claims that she was pregnant, bleeding, and having a miscarriage. Salva asked to go to the hospital more than ten times, but rather than getting her the medical attention she needed, Schnell mocked her, asking if people used cocaine in her native Sudan. Thirty-five minutes after the initial stop, Salva was jailed. The next morning, she was taken by ambulance to a hospital, where she delivered a premature baby who subsequently died.[19]

Both officers were fired for that incident in 2008, and Salva won a $750,000 settlement from the city.[20] By 2016, Schnell had been hired by two other police departments in Missouri, according to the *New York Times*. The last was a small police force in a town called Independence.

In 2004, Sean Sullivan was a police officer in a small Oregon town when he was caught kissing a ten-year-old girl on the mouth. He was charged, fired, and barred from ever working as a police officer again.

Just three months later, Sullivan was hired as the police chief in Cedar Vale, Kansas. While working there, Sullivan allegedly repeated the behavior that got him fired in Oregon. He was investigated after suspicion arose that he was in a sexual relationship with an underaged girl, and was eventually convicted on charges including criminal conspiracy and burglary. As of 2016, Sullivan was imprisoned in Washington State on other charges.

As for Pantaleo, his disciplinary file was hidden from the public for six years after his chokehold helped kill Eric Garner. The public didn't get to see Pantaleo's prior record until June 2020, when the New York state legislature repealed Section 50-a of the state's Civil Rights Law, which shielded police disciplinary records from public view.

A total of seventeen complaints were filed against Pantaleo with New York City's Civilian Complaint Review Board (CCRB) from 2009 to 2014.[21] Those complaints resulted in eight cases being opened against Pantaleo, including the case involving Eric's death. Three of those complaints were considered substantiated by the CCRB.

One of the substantiated complaints involved a 2011 vehicle stop and search where Pantaleo allegedly abused his power. Pantaleo received "instructions" as a punishment, according to his disciplinary record.

In 2012, Pantaleo was alleged to have abused his power while stopping and searching a pedestrian. That case resulted in a departmental disciplinary trial that found Pantaleo guilty. He forfeited two vacation days as punishment.

Perhaps, in another line of work, where mistakes, incompetence, or abuse could result in a loss of money, a worker could be given another opportunity. But bad police officers cost people their lives, and they simply cannot be allowed to return to positions where they are free to kill unarmed people of color like Eric Garner with impunity.

Daniel Pantaleo had a history of abusing his authority even before his actions cost Eric Garner his life. Many of those who defended him knew that history, and yet they tirelessly worked to reinstate him.

For Eric, for his children, and for all of us, this must never be allowed to happen again.

THE DEMAND

Make all police disciplinary and dismissal records public so that dangerous officers who are fired by one department cannot be hired by another, and create a federal database of former officers that departments can use to conduct thorough and mandatory background checks on all applicants.

6

ALTON STERLING

THE CASE FOR CHANGING FEDERAL LAW

IT WAS AFTER MIDNIGHT ON JULY 5, 2016, WHEN ALTON Sterling walked into the Triple S Food Mart in North Baton Rouge to buy a soft drink. He joked with his friend, store owner Abdullah Muflahi, a Yemeni immigrant who'd known the Black father of five for about six years. After a few minutes of conversation, Alton walked back outside to sell the CDs that had earned him the moniker The CD Man.

The jovial back-and-forth between the two men would be their last. In a few minutes, Alton Sterling would be dead, and his friend Abdullah Muflahi, one of several eyewitnesses, would call it murder.

Muflahi said that Alton Sterling had a handgun that night. Not because he planned to victimize anyone, but because he was concerned about becoming a victim himself.

"His friends also sell CDs at different locations," Muflahi later told NBC News. "They'd been getting robbed lately, so he felt that he needed something to protect himself if anything was to happen to him."[1]

According to numerous reports, Alton was approached by a seemingly homeless man who aggressively and repeatedly asked him for money. When Alton warned him off, the man, whose name was John Young, called 911 and told a police dispatcher that there was someone in front of the Triple S store selling CDs with a gun in his pocket.

"He pulled it on me and told me, 'You can't hang around here bro, you've got to move around,'" the man said during the call.[2]

After giving the dispatcher a description, the man repeated that Alton had a gun.

"The police know how to handle it," the dispatcher told him. "They're going to be on the way out."

The first policeman on the scene was Officer Howie Lake II, a white man. He got out of his car and walked up to Alton as he was selling CDs to two women outside the store.

"Could you please put your hands on that car right quick?" Lake said.[3]

"What'd I do?" Alton asked as Lake guided him toward a nearby sedan.

That's when a second officer, Blane Salamoni, also white, arrived on the scene. With an aggressiveness that investigators would later say served to escalate the situation, he quickly grabbed Alton around his head and drew his weapon.

"Don't fucking move or I'll shoot your fucking ass, bitch!" Salamoni screamed. "Put your fucking hands on the car! Put your hands on the car or I'll shoot you in your fucking head, you understand me? Don't you fucking move, you hear me?"[4] The officers slammed Alton against the car, and as Alton began to struggle, telling the officers that they were hurting his arm, Salamoni said to Lake, "Tase his ass!"

Alton, still facing the car, raised his hands slightly in a gesture of surrender as the two officers backed away. Lake deployed his Taser, hitting Alton in the back. The jolt made Alton's knees buckle and he fell to the ground before scrambling back to his feet. At Salamoni's urging, Lake deployed the Taser again.

Alton then stood with his arms outstretched, asking the officers what he'd done. Salamoni ran toward him and tackled him, ramming him into an SUV and then twisting him into the car before the three men tumbled to the ground.

Salamoni shouted, "He's got a gun!" Lake pinned Alton's left arm beneath his knee, and Salamoni yelled, "He's going for the gun!"

Two seconds later, Salamoni made good on his earlier threats. He shot Alton in the chest three times, and as the mortally wounded man tried to get up, Salamoni pumped another three bullets into his back.

Horrified, a woman filming the shooting in a nearby car broke down in tears. The man who was sitting next to her profanely expressed his shock. Abdullah Muflahi, the store owner, filmed on a cell phone as his store's surveillance system recorded a separate video of the scene.

Then, while Alton lay bleeding, Lake removed a loaded .38-caliber handgun from Alton's pocket. As he did so, John Young, the man who'd made the initial call to 911, was back on the phone with a dispatcher.

"They got it," Young said. "They got him, too. . . . They got that pistol."

"The police got him?" the dispatcher asked. "They're out there now?"

By then, Young had hung up, and as Lake instructed onlookers to stay back, Salamoni, with his gun still drawn, searched Alton's pockets. As he did so, Salamoni spit vitriol at the dying man.

"Stupid motherfucker," Salamoni said repeatedly as cash fell from Alton's pockets.

Lake radioed for EMS after the shooting, telling the dispatcher that both officers were okay, but the suspect was down.

"Where's the gun, Howie?" Salamoni asked Lake.

"It's in my car," Lake said. "I got it."

Watching from inside the store as his friend's life slipped away, store owner Abdullah Muflahi put the phone he'd used to record the shooting into his pocket.

"I knew they would take it from me if they knew I had it," Muflahi later told *The Guardian*. "They took my security camera videos. They told me they had a warrant, but didn't show me one. So I kept this video for myself. Otherwise, what proof do I have?"[5]

About ninety seconds after the shooting, Lake went to his car to get some gloves. When he came back to Alton's body, Lake told Salamoni, "I don't want to handcuff the dude."

"Fuck it," Salamoni said. "Just let him be."

Federal officials quickly took over the investigation into Alton Sterling's death, snatching the case from a Louisiana criminal justice system beset by structural racism and conflicts of interest.

Louisiana's then recently elected Democratic governor, John Bel Edwards, who is white, preached unity in the wake of Alton's death, but he came from a family of police officers. His brother, father, grandfather, and great-grandfather all served as sheriffs in Tangipahoa Parish, where Edwards was raised, while another brother was chief of police in the parish of Independence. Just months before Alton was killed, Edwards signed a controversial statute that made it a hate crime to attack police. It was a cynical response to the Black Lives Matter movement, and in a snarky bit of racist payback, the legislation was dubbed the "Blue Lives Matter" law.

Just as police had a firm grip on state politics, they also had control of Baton Rouge. A small city of 227,000[6] where a history of brutality and white supremacy created a toxic relationship between police and the Black community, Baton Rouge in 2016 was a place where a few people held immense power. Blane Salamoni—the officer who opened fire after claiming he saw Alton reaching for his gun—knew that well. He was born into a family that held sway in the Baton Rouge Police Department.

Salamoni's mother was the department's violent crime and crime scene commander, while his father commanded a special operations unit. Both parents had worked extensively with Hillar C. Moore III, East Baton Rouge's white district attorney. Moore's relationship to the Salamonis was so close that he immediately recused himself from the investigation into Alton's death.

"It is my determination as district attorney that given the history of a long and close working relationship with the parents of one of the officers involved in this shooting, there would always be questions of my partiality," Moore said in a ten-page report outlining his reason for recusing himself. "I state explicitly that this decision does not change my office's history of continuing to prosecute any local law enforcement officer responsible for violating our criminal laws. As we have always done, however, we will recuse ourselves when I have relationships that prevent me from handling the matter."[7]

Of course, Moore's recusal had little meaning since the district attorney's office would not have access to investigative materials until the federal investigation was complete.

Still, local officials had access to something that may have been more important—Blane Salamoni's record. And, just like New York officials hid the disciplinary record of Daniel Pantaleo, the police officer who choked Eric Garner, the Baton Rouge Police Department held on to facts about Salamoni that would have given the public a better idea of who he was and why his history mattered.

Salamoni, according to a Baton Rouge police chief and a police department lawyer, should have never been hired in the first place. Having been arrested in 2009 for physically assaulting a woman at a bar in downtown

Baton Rouge, Salamoni failed to disclose the arrest on his employment application. The arrest should have disqualified him from being hired as a police officer anywhere, but certainly in Baton Rouge, where he had been arrested. It's unclear why, in spite of the fact that officers in the department had to know about the arrest, he was hired just three years later.

Once he joined the department in 2012, Salamoni's behavior escalated. Baton Rouge police chief Murphy Paul said that shooting Alton Sterling was part of a well-documented pattern of "unprofessional behavior, police violence, marginalization, polarization and implicit bias by a man who should have never ever worn this uniform."[8]

That behavior included regular use of profanity and unnecessary force at work, and his relationships with his coworkers were also strained. Police lawyer Leo Hamilton said Salamoni had a "blow-up" with a fellow officer that was so intense it prompted another officer to say that if the department didn't do something about Salamoni, he could "eventually kill someone."

In 2016, when he shot Alton Sterling six times, Salamoni did just that.

Unfortunately, the Baton Rouge Police Department didn't reveal Salamoni's violent history until three years after he killed Alton. For those of us who work outside the criminal justice system, that might sound shocking, but hiding an officer's past incidents of misconduct is not unusual in these cases, especially when the officers are white and the victims are Black.

The NYPD and prosecutors used state law to keep Officer Daniel Pantaleo's disciplinary record hidden from the public for years after he killed Eric Garner. And while that law has since been repealed, about half the states still have laws that allow the disciplinary records of law enforcement officers to remain confidential, according to the Innocence Project. "In some states," writes the Innocence Project's Rebecca Brown, "the law explicitly bars these records from public view, while in others, police agencies hide these records under ambiguous legal precedents, making true accountability impossible."[9]

In short, concealing police discipline records is a systemically racist policy that allows abusive officers to repeatedly and secretly harm Black people. But in racist systems, anyone can be the abuser, regardless of skin color, and some officers have proved that in the most abhorrent ways.

One of them is Gerald Goines, a Black Houston narcotics officer who made thousands of arrests that came under review after prosecutors found inconsistencies in Goines's statements. In one such case, which was eerily reminiscent of the police shooting of Breonna Taylor, prosecutors alleged that Goines lied to get a no-knock warrant, and a couple died in their home as a result. A Houston judge also concluded that Goines likely lied about a ten-dollar drug deal for which he arrested George Floyd in 2004. George served ten months for that lie, and after he moved from Texas to Minnesota, he was killed by a Minneapolis police officer who had eighteen hidden disciplinary complaints prior to killing George. Those complaints only came to light after George was dead.

That's not unusual either. In many cases, according to Rebecca Brown, by the time an officer's history of misconduct comes to light, "communities may have endured preventable abuse on the streets while others may have been wrongfully incarcerated for years."

But just as police departments work hard to hide the disciplinary records of the officers involved in shootings, false arrests, and other abuses, they are diligent in dragging the names of Black victims through the mud. Alton Sterling was no exception.

A journalist at the *Baltimore Sun* reported that Baton Rouge officials were offering copies of Alton's arrest record to the media for $148 just a day after he was killed by Salamoni.[10]

Spanning forty-six pages, the record painted an ugly picture. It showed convictions for illegal weapons possession, battery, carnal knowledge of a teenager, possession of stolen property, disturbing the peace, and domestic abuse. Alton also was convicted for failing to register as a sex offender.

Releasing Alton's record right after he was killed by a police officer, whose violent behavior made even his colleagues wary, was meant to paint Alton as someone unworthy of public sympathy. It was meant to portray him as someone who deserved his fate. In sum, it was meant to protect the police.

Such tactics are common in these cases. In Ferguson, after Officer Darren Wilson shot and killed Michael Brown, police immediately released video of the teen taking cigarillos from a store. In New York, after Officer Daniel Pantaleo killed Eric Garner, police were quick to point out that the father of six had previously been arrested dozens of times—mostly for selling loose, untaxed cigarettes. In cases where the murder victim has no such record, police have sometimes tried to manufacture one.

That's what happened after police botched a raid and killed Breonna Taylor, an emergency room technician with no criminal record. As public outrage over Breonna's death grew, Breonna's former boyfriend, a convicted drug dealer named Jamarcus Glover, said police and prosecutors offered him a lighter sentence on pending drug charges if he would implicate Breonna in his drug enterprise. Glover and a lawyer produced a document called a plea sheet to corroborate their claim. Prosecutors claimed it was only a draft document, but Glover said he refused to accept the deal.[11]

Those who knew Alton also refused to go along with the police narrative. Instead of the hardened criminal that law enforcement portrayed him to be, his family and friends described Alton as a man who'd made mistakes but was trying to get his life on track. They said he was a gentle giant, an asthmatic who didn't present a threat to anyone, especially the police.

"I have no reason why the police feel threatened by Alton but his body size and the color of his skin," one of his cousins told NBC News.[12]

Others seemed to share that sentiment.

Abdullah Muflahi, who filmed Salamoni killing Alton outside his store, told NBC News that his friend was a nice guy. "Always smiling, always happy, always joking around with people. Never seen him get into fights with anybody, never seen him get into any, kind of, even arguments out there with people."

Beyond his friendly demeanor, those who knew him said Alton was funny. His aunt, Sandra Sterling, who raised him after he lost his mother at the age of ten, told the *Times-Picayune* that Alton loved to make people laugh.

On the night he died, that's what Alton was doing. He laughed with his friend Abdullah in the Triple S Food Mart. Then he went outside to sell his CDs—a hustle that gave him freedom.

He'd been home from prison for about six months at the time, having served a five-year sentence with credit for time served after pleading guilty to carrying a gun while in possession of a controlled substance.

Clearly, Alton was not a man without blemish, and he never claimed to be, but he was determined to stay home and take care of his five children. That was his focus, and selling CDs and DVDs allowed him to do so legally. Much like Eric Garner, who sold loose cigarettes to provide for his family, Alton found a product that he could use to earn the money he needed to be a legitimate breadwinner. By all accounts, Alton was good at it.

Described by those who knew him as a people person who could get along with anyone, Alton paid ninety dollars a week for a room in a boarding house on West Brookstown Drive in Baton Rouge. The house was a place where men like him went to start over after past mistakes, and Alton made the best of it.

He was good in the kitchen and was one of the few men who would cook for the other residents. Alton was well known for his red beans and rice, and Asha Bennie, who managed the boarding house, noticed something else about him.

His family, including the mother of his children, would often bring his children to see him at the house. So yes, he was a man who'd made many mistakes. Chief among them was his conviction for unlawful carnal knowledge of a minor when he was around twenty years old. Because of that conviction, which earned him a label as a sex offender, Alton had a hard time finding housing or holding down a job. Still, he was working part-time as a cook and selling CDs on the side before he was killed by the police.

After they killed his body, they assassinated his character. First, they widely disseminated his criminal record. Years later they released a toxicology report that sought to portray drugs as a contributing factor in his death, much like police did in the death of George Floyd.

But in the interim, there was anger. Not just about the videos that showed the out-of-control behavior of Officer Blane Salamoni. There was a cumulative anger building up about the police killings of Black people all over the country. Every day there was another video, and even when there wasn't a video, there were deeply etched images of injustice.

The names just kept coming: Rekia Boyd, Sandra Bland, Eric Garner, Freddie Gray, Tamir Rice, Walter Scott, Michael Brown, Jamar Clark, Sam Dubose, Akai Gurley, Jeremy McDole.

Rarely did the Black community see justice in such cases, so when videos surfaced of Alton being pinned down and shot by police, the protests were different. And when the aftermath of a Minneapolis police officer shooting Philando Castile was livestreamed the next day, the level of anger instantly rose, and the police response did too.

Black Lives Matter protesters, who were largely peaceful, were met by Baton Rouge police officers in full riot gear. Between July 8 and July 11, the department arrested 185 protesters.[13] That's more than Capitol Police and federal officials arrested on the day thousands of right-wing insurgents violently stormed the US Capitol.

In fact, the Baton Rouge response to peaceful protesters was so heavy-handed that the department and the city were later sued by the American Civil Liberties Union of Louisiana and activist DeRay Mckesson, who said police responded to the protesters in a "militarized and aggressive manner."[14]

However, the protests were not confined to Baton Rouge, and there were individual actors who had no interest in participating in the nonviolent marches taking place in cities across the country.

On July 7, as a peaceful protest was ending in Dallas, Micah Xavier Johnson, a twenty-five-year-old military veteran who'd served in Afghanistan, opened fire on police. He killed five and wounded seven others. Before police killed Johnson with a robotic bomb device, he told negotiators that he wanted to kill white police officers in retaliation for the murders of Alton Sterling and Philando Castile.

Ten days later, Gavin Long, a twenty-nine-year-old Black man from Kansas City, Missouri, shot and killed two Baton Rouge police officers and a sheriff's deputy. He wounded three more officers before police killed him.

To be clear, that kind of carnage is not the norm when Blacks protest police killings. But when people have no expectation of justice and no real means to attain it, violence can sometimes result.

Black people had no reason to believe there would be justice for Alton or Philando. But at least the Black community of Baton Rouge could hold onto the hope that a federal investigation would be harder for local officials to rig.

As it turned out, their hope was misplaced. No one had to rig the DOJ's investigation of Alton's death. The burden of proof is so high in federal prosecutions of police officers that convictions are incredibly rare.

When the DOJ investigates civil rights violations by police officers, it is governed by Title 18 of the US Code. In Chapter 13, Section 242, the law says, "Whoever, under color of any law . . . willfully subjects any person in any State . . . to the deprivation of any rights . . . protected by the Constitution or laws of the United States, or to different punishments . . . by reason of his color, or race . . . shall be fined . . . or imprisoned not more than one year, or both."[15]

If the person who acts under color of law to deprive someone of their civil rights kills them in the process, the offender can receive a much harsher sentence, up to and including the death penalty. On the surface, the law seems fairly clear, but there is one word in the US Code that consistently saves officers who kill from being federally prosecuted. That word is "willfully."

In essence, prosecutors seeking federal civil rights convictions against a police officer must go beyond proving that the officer deprived someone of their civil rights based on race. They have to also prove that the officer meant to do so and did it based on a clear sense of racism. That means prosecutors must find a way to do what would normally be impossible—climb into the officer's head and find out exactly what they were thinking.

In the case of Officer Blane Salamoni, that should not have been difficult, because he told the world exactly what he was thinking from the moment he arrived at the scene.

"Don't fucking move or I'll shoot your fucking ass, bitch!" Salamoni screamed while aggressively grabbing Alton's head. "Put your fucking hands on the car! Put your hands on the car or I'll shoot you in your fucking head, you understand me? Don't you fucking move, you hear me?"

Louisiana attorney general Jeff Landry, a white man who himself is a former police officer, later said that in uttering these words, Salamoni issued a "loud aggressive verbal command and [threatened] to shoot him if he [did] not comply. This level of verbal escalation [appeared] to be momentarily effective as the officers [were] able to direct Mr. Sterling to the vehicle and attempt to place him in custody."[16]

The truth is, Alton was already walking toward the vehicle before Salamoni grabbed him by the head, drew his weapon, and threatened to kill him. But even if that were not the case, Salamoni's death threat should've served as a red flag for investigators.

That's why the American Civil Liberties Union of Louisiana called the decision not to charge either officer a travesty and denounced Landry's description of Salamoni's actions. "A death threat is not an acceptable warning," ACLU of Louisiana assistant director Colleen Kane Gielskie wrote about the case. "And, coming from police and directed at Black and brown people, death is too often the result."[17]

But rather than consider the deadly threats issued by the officers—and particularly Salamoni—DOJ investigators focused on three questions: Did Alton Sterling reach for his weapon? Were the actions of the officers reasonable? Was the second series of shots a violation of the Fourth Amendment?

In an investigation that moved quickly by DOJ standards, federal prosecutors took less than a year to declare that there was insufficient evidence to charge either officer with violating Alton Sterling's civil rights.

The US attorney for the Middle District of Louisiana, Corey Amundson, also a white man, issued a statement explaining the decision. In it, DOJ officials conceded that while numerous videos of the incident "do not show Sterling's right hand at the time those shots were fired," they do "show that Sterling's right hand was not under Officer Salamoni's control."[18]

That statement makes no sense. If Alton Sterling's hand was not visible, how can anyone definitively say that it wasn't under Salamoni's control? It is possible that Alton's right arm could have been under Salamoni's knee, just like Alton's left arm was pinned under Officer Lake's knee.

"The evidence also cannot establish that Sterling was not reaching for a gun when Officer Salamoni yelled that Sterling was doing so," said the Justice Department's statement.

Again, there is ample room for doubt here. Given that Salamoni yelled that Alton was reaching for a gun, why was Salamoni the only one to fire? Why didn't Officer Lake fire as well? Perhaps more importantly, why did Justice Department investigators dismiss the statements of two witnesses who said they could see Alton's right hand and that his right hand was not in his pocket?

The Justice Department said the witness statements were inconsistent and didn't coincide with the videos, but if the videos didn't show Alton's right hand, how do we know the statements don't line up with the video evidence?

On the question of whether the officers' actions were reasonable, the Justice Department cited the opinions of two use-of-force experts. "The experts emphasized that the officers were responding to a call that someone matching Sterling's description had brandished a weapon and threatened another person; that Sterling was large and strong; and that Sterling was failing to follow orders and was struggling with the officers," the statement said.

It continued, "The experts noted that the officers also attempted to control Sterling through multiple less-than-lethal techniques before ultimately using lethal force in response to Officer Salamoni's perception that Sterling was attempting to use a gun."

The statement is an admission that Salamoni—an officer whose troubling disciplinary record was unknown to the public—was the only one who perceived that Alton was attempting to use a gun.

Perhaps more troubling, the Justice Department disregarded the videos in deciding not to consider the second series of shots fired by Salamoni as a violation of Alton's Fourth Amendment rights, which protect Americans against unreasonable search and seizure.

"Although the videos show that Sterling's right hand was not in or near his right pocket, Sterling was continuing to move, even after being shot three times and being told again not to move by Officer Lake," the Justice Department said.

"Meanwhile, the officers were behind Sterling, and Officer Salamoni was lying on the ground, facing Sterling's back. Given these circumstances, the evidence cannot establish beyond a reasonable doubt that it did not appear to Officer Salamoni that Sterling was reaching for his pocket. Nor could the Department prove that the officer's conduct was willful."

There's that word again—"willful." It functions almost as an escape clause for officers who brazenly violate the civil rights of Black people. That word served as the linchpin for the federal decision not to charge Lake or Salamoni for killing Alton Sterling, but there were no words to alleviate the pain felt by Alton's family.

"It's like, we waited all this time for nothing," said Sandra Sterling, the aunt who raised Alton as her own. "And as we were going through the process, I kept asking them, 'What happens if they come back with this decision?' . . . They said, 'Well, it will be worth the wait.' But no, it's not worth the wait. It's not worth the wait. All this was for nothing."[19]

"It just hurts so bad," she added in an interview with ABC News. "It's a horrible pain. . . . It's like going back to the first day all over again."

Amundson, the US attorney said, "There are no winners here, and there are no victories for anybody. A man has died, a father, a nephew has died. My heart goes out to the family. . . . There simply isn't enough evidence to proceed with the federal charge."[20]

Except there was a winner in the Alton Sterling case. The winner was injustice. That's why the threshold for convicting police officers on federal civil rights charges must change.

Let's be clear. While there were myriad issues with the state investigation led by Louisiana attorney general Jeff Landry, a conservative former police officer who refused to step aside for an independent prosecutor, his investigation essentially served as a rubber stamp for the federal decision. With all the familial connections to law enforcement at the state and local levels, no one truly expected to get justice there.

However, Alton's family, and indeed all of us who sought true justice, were hoping that the federal civil rights investigation would yield a better result. But just as federal prosecutors failed to charge Darren Wilson in the shooting death of Michael Brown in Ferguson, Missouri, and failed to charge Daniel Pantaleo in the choking death of Eric Garner on a Staten Island Street corner, federal prosecutors failed to charge Howie Lake or Blane Salamoni in Alton's death.

Videos or not, witnesses or not, history or not, federal prosecutors don't convict white police officers in the shootings of Black people. That's not a coincidence. That's systemic racism, and it turns on a single idea in the federal statute—that the violation of the victim's civil rights must be willful.

Perhaps, in the case of Officer Lake, who never fired his service weapon, the decision not to charge him with willfully violating Alton's civil rights can be justified. However, for Blane Salamoni, the son of high-ranking officers in a department that later said it never should have hired him, the question of willfulness could not have been clearer.

When your colleagues say your conduct is so out of control that you will eventually kill somebody, that points to willfulness. When you have a long record of use of force and implicit bias that your superiors later acknowledge, that is a great indicator of willfulness. When you threaten to kill someone seconds after arriving on the scene, and then you do it, that, surely, demonstrates willfulness.

Shamefully, Salamoni's record was not exposed to the public until 2019—a year after Salamoni was fired and the DOJ declined to file charges in Alton Sterling's death. But under the current federal standards, even if his record was known to the public, charging him would have been nearly impossible, and the numbers bear that out.

A *Pittsburgh Tribune-Review* study of over thirteen thousand police misconduct cases submitted to the DOJ found that no charges were filed in 96 percent of them.[21]

That must change, because there will be more Alton Sterlings, there will be more Blane Salamonis, and if we do not act, there will be more injustice.

There is currently federal legislation pending that would bring about the needed change. It's called the George Floyd Justice in Policing Act, and while it's named after George Floyd, it is exactly the kind of legislation that would have made all the difference in gaining justice for Alton Sterling.

The wide-ranging bill contains language that would do the following: limit qualified immunity so that police officers can be sued for their on-duty actions; authorize the DOJ to issue subpoenas in pattern and practice investigations; and lower the criminal intent standard—from willful to knowing or reckless—to convict a law enforcement officer for misconduct in a federal prosecution.

In heartbreaking videos, it's clear that Officer Blane Salamoni is the only one who claimed to see Alton Sterling reaching for a gun. It's clear that Officer Salamoni pumped six bullets into a man who was pinned to the ground. And while it may not be possible to prove that he willfully violated Alton's civil rights, it's clear that he knowingly or recklessly did so. From the moment he arrived, Salamoni behaved like a man who intended to kill, and in the end, he acted on that intent.

Activists must pressure federal legislators to pass the George Floyd Justice in Policing Act, because of all the things that George and Alton had in common, this bill will be the most impactful.

THE DEMAND

The federal law governing the prosecution of police officers for civil rights violations must be changed so that the standard for charging officers is reachable, realistic, and relevant. Therefore, we demand that the standard for charging a police officer with violating the civil rights of a civilian be changed from willfully doing so, to "knowingly or recklessly" doing so. We demand that the George Floyd Justice in Policing Act be passed.

7

TAMIR RICE

THE CASE FOR INDEPENDENT PROSECUTORS

IT WAS A SATURDAY AFTERNOON IN NOVEMBER 2014, AND Cleveland's West Side still bore the remnants of a recent snowstorm as a twelve-year-old Black boy named Tamir Rice played alone near a gazebo at Cudell Commons.

The park was familiar to Tamir. Not only because his mother had recently moved the family to a nearby rowhouse, but also because Tamir and his sister, Tajai, had been coming to the park and the adjacent recreation center for years.

Located at Detroit Avenue and West Boulevard, Cudell Recreation Center is in a community that some might call blighted, but for Tamir it was a safe space. In fact, it was one of two places where he spent the most time. At the recreation center, he played basketball on the courts. Across the park, at Marion C. Seltzer Elementary, he played jokes on his friends.

At five feet seven and 195 pounds, the sixth grader was big for his age, but his round face was that of a child. It was a face that was often fixed in an impish grin—the face of a boy who was mischievous enough to prank classmates at school, yet nurturing enough to take care of younger relatives at family gatherings.

Those who knew him told the *New York Times* that Tamir was the kind of child who would address his elders as "Sir" and "Ma'am," but on that November afternoon, he was labeled as something else altogether, and it all started with a toy.

Usually, when Tamir wasn't playing basketball or table games at the recreation center, he played games on his mother's old cell phone. But that day, he ran into a friend who had an Airsoft pellet gun his dad had purchased at Walmart. It was a replica of a Colt M1911 semi-automatic pistol, and it looked real, especially after a repair left the gun without the orange tip that distinguished it from an actual handgun.

Tamir and his friend made a trade that day. Tamir let his friend borrow the phone, and his friend let Tamir use the pellet gun. Playing with the toy pistol was a different experience for Tamir, because his mother, Samaria, didn't allow him to play with guns of any kind. Not water guns, not cap pistols, not anything that even had the look of a sidearm. She was always concerned that someone might mistake a toy gun for a real one.

But on that November afternoon, Tamir finally had a chance to play with a forbidden toy, and like any child, he took advantage of the moment. As Tamir paced back and forth in the park, pointing the toy at the air, and sometimes at passersby, a man sat on a bench, drinking beer and watching him. The man was waiting for a bus, but as he watched Tamir playing with the realistic-looking pistol, he grew concerned enough to call the police, and in that moment, Samaria Rice's worse nightmare was realized.

"I'm sitting in the park at West Boulevard by the West Boulevard Rapid Transit Station," the man calmly told a 911 dispatcher. "And there's a guy in here with a pistol, you know, it's probably fake, but he's like pointing it at everybody."[1]

In the recording of the call, one thing stands out. There is no sense of urgency in the caller's voice. He didn't speak like someone who feared that a man with a gun was about to kill him or anyone else. In fact, his tone was decidedly casual, as if he knew that this was no real emergency, and as he spoke to the dispatcher, he made sure to include the detail that made him feel that way.

"The guy keeps pulling it in and out of his pants," he told the dispatcher. "It's probably fake, but you know what, he's scaring the shit out of people.

"He's sitting on the swing right now, but he keeps pulling it in and out of his pants and pointing it at people," the caller said. "Probably a juvenile, you know?"

There was a pause at the other end, as if the dispatcher was trying to decide whether this casual call about a man with a gun was genuine.

"Hello?" the caller said.

"Do you know the guy?" the dispatcher asked.

"No, I do not."

"Okay, we'll send the police, okay?"

"I'm getting ready to leave," the caller said, "but he's right here by the youth center or whatever . . . And he keeps pulling it in and out of his pants. I don't know if it's real or not."

"Okay, we'll send a car over there," the dispatcher said. "Thank you."

However, the recording of the subsequent exchanges between dispatchers and police don't include the caller's repeated warnings that the guy with the gun could be a juvenile, or that the gun might indeed be a fake.

"In the park by the youth center is a Black male sitting on the swings," the new dispatcher said. "He's wearing a camouflage hat, a gray jacket with black sleeves. . . . He keeps pulling a gun out of his pants and pointing it at people."

"How many calls are you getting for that?" another dispatcher asked.

"Just the one so far."

When the call went out over the air, Officer Frank Garmback and his trainee, rookie officer Timothy Loehmann, were finishing up a false alarm call. The officers, both white, rushed to respond to the priority one call of a Black male with a gun. Garmback was the veteran officer, and he was driving. He decided to go in aggressively.

Rather than pulling up on the street or on the sidewalk that ran along the edge of the grass near the gazebo, Garmback barreled through the park, driving on grass still damp from the recent snow. In doing so, the training officer disregarded normal tactics. He didn't let dispatchers know when they arrived on the scene. Nor did he wait for backup, and in a move that would've threatened all of their lives had Tamir been a man with a real gun, Garmback drove the car so close to Tamir that it skidded in the grass, stopping four to seven feet from Tamir as the child walked toward the police car with his hands near his waist.

Before the car came to a complete stop, rookie officer Timothy Loehmann jumped out with his gun drawn and later claimed that in that moment he told Rice three times to show him his hands. Video of the incident proved it would've been virtually impossible for Loehmann to give three warnings since Loehmann fired two shots less than two seconds after he and Garmback arrived.

One of the bullets Loehmann fired hit Tamir in the torso from point blank range. The boy dropped to the ground, bleeding as the officers pointed guns at him. In the chaotic moments that followed, Garmback got on the radio and called for help.

"Radio, shots fired," Garmback said. "Male down. Black male, maybe 20. Black revolver, black handgun by him. Send EMS this way, and a roadblock."

Ninety seconds later, Tamir's fourteen-year-old sister, Tajai, ran to the scene and tried to get to her brother's side, but before she could do so, Loehmann and Garmback tackled and handcuffed her. She was later put in the back of a police car to watch as her brother lay bleeding on the ground.

As precious minutes ticked by, neither Garmback nor Loehmann nor any of the Cleveland officers who arrived on the scene offered medical help to Tamir. When Samaria Rice showed up demanding to see what had happened to her son, the police threatened to lock her up if she didn't calm down.

Four minutes after Tamir was shot, an FBI agent who happened to be in the area was the first to render first aid of any kind. Still, the clock kept ticking.

It was eight minutes after the shooting when paramedics finally arrived. Another five minutes passed before they lifted Tamir onto a stretcher and transported him to MetroHealth Medical Center in Cleveland. Doctors there performed a surgical procedure that included a closure of the inferior vena cava proximal to the gunshot wound. However, they couldn't save him.

Tamir was pronounced dead at 12:54 a.m. on Sunday.

According to the autopsy from Cuyahoga County medical examiner Dr. Thomas P. Gilson, the cause of death was a single gunshot wound to the torso with "injuries of major vessel, intestines and pelvis." The manner of death was homicide.[2]

The silent surveillance video was everywhere. Two white officers speeding up to a Black child, flinging open a car door, and killing him in less than two seconds. The resultant rage was exacerbated by the news that they'd handcuffed Tamir's fourteen-year-old sister for daring to come to his aid. That rage was married to grief as the world watched a video loop of a Black child being gunned down again and again.

In Cleveland, Black protesters were joined by whites and other allies who were outraged by the police killing of a sixth grader. They took to the streets, shouting for justice and holding signs bearing slogans like "The whole damn system is guilty!"

On the heels of the 2014 police killings of unarmed Black victims like Dontre Hamilton in Milwaukee, Eric Garner in New York, John Crawford in Dayton, Michael Brown in Ferguson, Ezell Ford in California, and Tanisha Anderson, who died less than ten days before Tamir in Cleveland, it wasn't only the system that was guilty. The country itself was guilty, because the Black people who were killed at the hands of white police officers weren't isolated to one area or one age group. It was men, women, and children, gay and straight. And the carnage showed no signs of abating. But even in the face of the heinous act of a police officer shooting a child, the system in Cleveland didn't seek justice. It sought to protect itself.

Tamir hadn't been dead for a full day when Cleveland police and their representatives started to craft a narrative about the shooting. As in other shootings, the police union was aggressive in its defense of the officers' actions, and its leaders were loose with the facts.

Cleveland Police Patrolmen's Association president Jeffrey Follmer, who is white, told the *Cleveland Plain Dealer* that when Garmback and Loehmann pulled up, they saw a few people sitting underneath the gazebo next to the recreation center and that the rookie officer, Timothy Loehmann, saw Tamir pick up a black gun from the table and put it in his waistband.

However, video of the incident clearly shows that Tamir was alone. There was no one else under the gazebo, and the toy gun was already in Tamir's waistband. It never appeared to be on the table.

The police union wasn't the only entity to say things that contradicted the evidence. The official departmental positions were questionable too.

A statement about the shooting from the Cleveland police department said, "Upon arrival on the scene, officers located the suspect and advised him to raise his hands. The suspect did not comply with the officers' orders and reached to his waistband for the gun. Shots were fired and the suspect was struck in the torso."[3]

That assertion was repeated by department commanders during a press conference.

"Yes, three commands were given to 'show your hands' by Officer Loehmann as he pulled up to the gazebo there," deputy police chief Ed Tomba told reporters. "They were out the door. His door was open as he pulled up and he was yelling at—yelling three commands. He yelled three times as they pulled up."[4]

Tomba, like the officers involved, is white.

But those in the Black community who saw the video, which did not include sound, remained unconvinced that the officers ever warned Tamir before they shot him.

"I mean, he had to be literally yelling out the window as the car drove up," Cleveland City Council member Jeffrey Johnson, who is Black, told Rev. Al Sharpton on MSNBC's *Politics Nation*. "And you know, we need to look at the veteran police officer who actually chose to put the vehicle two feet from Tamir, rather than further back so that they could get out and assess before they moved forward to determine the threat."[5]

Johnson said he believed both officers were to blame. Garmback for pulling up so close to Tamir and putting a rookie like Loehmann in a position to shoot, and Loehmann for shooting Tamir in less than two seconds. Perhaps more important than what Johnson did believe about the incident is what he and many others in Cleveland's Black community did not.

"We don't buy that they sat back and made these demands and Tamir ignored them," Johnson told Sharpton. "We don't believe Tamir had enough time to assess what was going on."

Still, Garmback and Loehmann persisted in claiming that Tamir ignored multiple commands before he was shot. Both men claimed in videotaped interviews with investigators from the Cleveland police department that their actions were justified.

"Show me your hands! Show me your hands! Show me your hands!" Frank Garmback told investigators while reenacting what he claimed Loehmann told Tamir right before Loehmann opened fire.[6]

"I can see through here the kid reaching, pulling a—" Garmback paused, as if to gather himself.

"Take your time," said one of the men who was interviewing him.

"I didn't know it was a kid," Garmback said, his voice cracking.

Loehmann, in a videotaped interview, echoed Garmback's story, telling investigators he had no choice but to shoot.

"At first you see him, you know, the male matching the description, but then you see the gun," Loehmann said. "And then, now, he's, you know, walking away, and now, you know, he's presenting the gun, and you know, he's pulling it out of his waistband. So, your levels are getting higher and higher and higher. And the threat just became incredible where, you know, I had to, you know, make the decision fast, because Frank and I were in immediate danger."[7]

In those same videotaped interviews, Garmback told investigators that after Tamir was shot, an FBI agent tried to communicate with the injured boy while rendering first aid.

"He's talking to the kid and the kid's looking at him, not saying much," Garmback said.

"Is he saying anything that you recall?" one of the investigators asked.

"No, nothing at all. No, he's—maybe moans. I get on radio and I'm telling them speed it up, speed it up . . . and I can see this kid's eyes rolling in the back of his head and he's barely breathing," Garmback said haltingly, his voice breaking.

But even after he broke down several times while explaining to investigators what happened, it wasn't Garmback whose emotional stability was in doubt. It was Loehmann.

The son of a New York police officer, Timothy Loehmann was eight months into his training with the Cleveland police department when he shot Tamir Rice. But Cleveland's wasn't the first department where Loehmann had problems as a trainee. In fact, Loehmann's experience in a previous department should have disqualified him from ever being hired in Cleveland.

In a 2012 letter, Deputy Chief Jim Polak of the Independence Police Department said Loehmann suffered from emotional immaturity. It was an issue that showed up repeatedly when Loehmann was a trainee in the small police force. It was especially evident when he was dealing with firearms.

In that letter, which was contained in Loehmann's Independence personnel file, Polak wrote that the officer was "distracted" and "weepy" during firearms qualification training.[8] "He could not follow simple directions, could not communicate clear thoughts nor recollections, and his handgun performance was dismal," Polak had written.

Loehmann told a supervisor that his emotional breakdown was brought on by a recent breakup with a girlfriend. But Polak made it clear in his letter that Loehmann's issues were about much more than a one-time incident. According to Polak, Loehmann's problems as a police trainee were grounded in a troubling pattern of emotional breakdowns and an unwillingness to follow instructions concerning everything from locking up his service weapon to wearing a bulletproof vest. Polak wrote in his letter,

> Patrolman Loehmann's inability to perform basic functions as instructed, and his inability to emotionally function because of a personal situation at home with an on and off again girlfriend leads one to believe that he would not be able to substantially cope, or make good decisions, during or resulting from any other stressful situation. Due to this dangerous loss of composure during live range training and his inability to manage this personal stress, I do not believe Patrolman Loehmann shows the maturity needed to work in our employment. Unfortunately, in law enforcement there are times when instructions need be followed to the letter, and I am under the impression Patrolman Loehmann, under certain circumstances, will not react in the way instructed.

Loehmann resigned before he could be fired. Then he tried and failed to join multiple law enforcement agencies before landing in Cleveland.

Officials in the Cleveland police department later said they never reviewed Loehmann's personnel file from Independence. However, one is left to wonder what they would have decided if they'd known that a deputy police chief in another department had determined that Loehmann "would not be able to substantially cope, or make good decisions, during or resulting from any other stressful situation."

Those words read like a warning—one that could have saved Tamir's life if they'd only been heeded by someone in a position of authority. Clearly, they were not, and now a boy is dead.

Tamir's death was about more than the decision to hire a police officer without fully vetting him. It was also about the actions of the training officer, the violent culture of Cleveland's police department, and the refusal of a white county prosecutor to hold either officer accountable.

That lack of criminal penalties for violent, often deadly policing in Cleveland was a pattern that had been in place for years.

■ ■ ■

More than a decade before Tamir was shot, a rash of police shootings led the DOJ to investigate the Cleveland police department. That investigation was the precursor to an agreement by the city to upgrade its guidelines on the use of force and better document such occurrences.

The changes that came as a result of that agreement didn't stick. In 2011 police were caught on video kicking a Black man named Edward Henderson in the head and breaking a bone in his face, even as Henderson was on the ground and not resisting.

The city paid $600,000 to Edwards in that case, but none of the officers involved were fired and none admitted wrongdoing.

Nearly two years later, some sixty Cleveland police cars engaged in a high-speed chase after mistaking the sound of a car backfiring for gunshots. When they caught up to the vehicle they were chasing, thirteen officers fired a total of 137 bullets into the car; the driver was struck twenty-three times, and the front seat passenger was struck twenty-four times.[9] Both Timothy Russell and Malissa Williams—the two unarmed Black people inside—were dead on the scene.

Only one officer, a white policeman named Michael Brelo, was charged with voluntary manslaughter in the case. Brelo, who jumped on the hood of the victims' car after it stopped and fired a barrage of forty-nine bullets through their windshield, claimed he did so because he feared for his life. Cuyahoga County Common Pleas Court judge John O'Donnell, who is also white, claimed that even though Brelo fired at least one fatal wound to Malissa Williams's chest, he couldn't determine that the other fatal shots came from Brelo's gun.

Cuyahoga County prosecutor Timothy McGinty handled the case, failing to win a conviction in a case where more than a hundred police officers contributed to the deaths of two unarmed Black people, and thirteen fired their weapons into their car.

David Malik, a prominent white civil rights attorney who has filed scores of lawsuits against the Cleveland police told the *New York Times* that policing in Cleveland is "a culture of no consequences."[10]

That is the context in which police and the Black community coexist in Cleveland. It is a hostile standoff where one side holds all the cards, and the other side holds on to grief. Yet there was something different about the killing of Tamir Rice—a child who was killed while playing in a park where his mother thought he was safe. It was an injury to parents everywhere. But more than that, it was a videotaped indication that the split-second decisions police claim to make are sometimes not decisions at all. They are simply reactions to Blackness—a deadly brand of implicit bias that says Black skin is a threat.

Days after Tamir was killed, a grand jury in Ferguson, Missouri, decided not to indict Darren Wilson, the white police officer who shot and killed unarmed Black teen Michael Brown. Protests erupted, and in that moment, the memories of Michael and Tamir were linked, because in the minds of those on fire for justice, the inferno that was Ferguson was quickly burning out, but Tamir was an ember of hope.

Still, the investigation of Tamir's shooting dragged on for months. Winter gave way to spring, and as summer came, the Black community grew weary of the lack of progress by Cuyahoga County prosecutor Timothy McGinty, the same white official who had failed to convict Michael Brelo.

A group of mostly Black citizens used an unusual Ohio law to petition the Cleveland Municipal Court to have officers Garmback and Loehmann arrested for killing Tamir. The law, which has been in effect in various forms since 1960, allows "a private citizen having knowledge of the facts" to start the charging process by filing an affidavit with the court. The filers argued that seeing the widely circulated video of Tamir's death gave them, and nearly everyone, knowledge of the facts.[11]

The petitioners included Dr. Jawanza Colvin, Bakari Kiwana, Edward Little, Julia Shearson, Rachelle Smith, Dr. R.A. Vernon, Dr. Rhonda Williams, and Joseph Worthy. In their affidavits, they accused Loehmann and Garmback of aggravated murder, murder, involuntary manslaughter, reckless homicide, negligent homicide, and dereliction of duty.

Judge Ronald B. Adrine, who is Black, ruled on their complaint in four days. In doing so, he made it clear that in addition to the affidavits, the footage of Tamir's death was at the center of his decision. In his ten-page ruling, Adrine wrote,

> The video in question in this case is notorious and hard to watch. After viewing it several times, this court is still thunderstruck by how quickly this event turned deadly. . . .
>
> The video depicts Rice approaching the Zone Car just as it pulls into

> the park but it does not appear to show him making any furtive movement prior to, or at, the moment he is shot. Again, because of the quality of the video, the young man's arms are barely visible, but they do not appear to be raised or outstretched. In the moments immediately before, and as the Zone Car approaches, the video does not display the toy gun in Tamir's hands. There appears to be little if any time reflected on the video for Rice to react or respond to any verbal or audible commands given from Loehmann and Garmback from their Zone Car between the time that they first arrived and the time that Rice was shot. Literally, the entire encounter is over in an instant.
>
> Beyond the videos presented as exhibits, each affidavit sets forth the statutory language of each offense alleged. It is unquestioningly sufficient to charge felony crimes in the words of the statutes.[12]

Judge Adrine recommended that the city or county prosecutor file charges against Garmback for negligent homicide and dereliction of duty and file charges against Loehmann for murder, involuntary manslaughter, reckless homicide, negligent homicide, and dereliction of duty.

Right after the ruling, Walter Madison, a lawyer for Tamir's family, told the *New York Times*, "The people made the system work for them. The onus now is on the government to act, and I don't think a prosecutor's office is going to defy a court."[13]

Madison was wrong. The city prosecutor's office responded to the ruling with a statement saying Cuyahoga County prosecutor Timothy McGinty would determine whether charges would be filed, and McGinty issued a statement making clear that he would not follow the court's recommendation. Instead, he would explore charges in Tamir's shooting using the same secret mechanism that St. Louis County prosecutor Robert McCulloch utilized in the police shooting of Michael Brown.

"This case, as with all other fatal use-of-deadly-force cases involving law enforcement officers, will go to the grand jury," McGinty said. "That has been the policy of this office since I was elected. Ultimately, the grand jury decides whether police officers are charged or not charged."

But McGinty left out a few key facts, the most important of which are these: The grand jury is a tool of the prosecutor, and while it's true that the grand jury decides whether to indict someone, it does so based solely on the information that's provided by the prosecutor. There is no cross-examination, no defense attorney, and no one to present an alternate point of view. Thus, grand jury decisions are shaped by prosecutors, and the process takes place in secret.

When a prosecutor does not want an indictment to take place, it doesn't, and just as America saw in the cases of Eric Garner and Alton Sterling and Michael Brown, Timothy McGinty did not appear to want the officers indicted, and he went to great lengths to obtain the desired outcome.

McGinty seemed determined that neither officer would face criminal charges for killing the twelve-year-old boy, and Tamir's family would later declare that McGinty was "abusing and manipulating the grand jury process to orchestrate a vote against indictment."[14]

McGinty spent his life in the Cleveland area and became a probation officer soon after earning a law degree from Cleveland State's John Marshall College of Law.

He later became an assistant prosecuting attorney in Cuyahoga County, handling a number of high-profile cases, including the 1989 prosecution of Ronnie Shelton, who was known as the West Side Rapist. McGinty then spent nearly two decades as a Cuyahoga County Common Pleas judge. He left the bench and was elected county prosecutor in 2012.

As a lifelong resident who'd spent decades holding prominent positions in criminal justice, McGinty knew what it took to win a conviction. In 2012, however, in his first year as county prosecutor, he learned firsthand the politics of prosecuting a police officer. He received swift backlash from police unions after he impaneled the grand jury that indicted Officer Michael Brelo for killing two unarmed Black civilians, and he was criticized in Cleveland's Black community after he failed to convict Brelo in what many thought would be an open-and-shut case.

Two years later, when the Tamir Rice case emerged in the midst of the Black Lives Matter movement, McGinty decided to go about things differently. From the outset, he moved slowly, and when he finally impaneled the grand jury, McGinty and his prosecutors acted like they were defending Officers Garmback and Loehmann rather than trying to win an indictment against them.

During the secret proceedings, McGinty publicly released several pieces of evidence that were being considered by the grand jury. This included a sheriff's report concluding that Loehmann had "no choice" but to shoot, statements from Loehmann and Garmback stating Tamir ignored warnings to show his hands while pulling the toy gun from his pants, and reports from three experts called by the prosecutors who concluded that Loehmann had "acted reasonably" because he perceived a "serious threat."[15]

Tamir's family accused McGinty of trying to lose the case, and blasted him for hiring what they called pro-police experts, later saying in a statement, "It is unheard of, and highly improper, for a prosecutor to hire 'experts' to try to exonerate the targets of a grand jury investigation. These are the sort of 'experts' we would expect the officer's criminal defense attorney to hire—not the prosecution."[16]

But the family went beyond criticism. They hired experts of their own. Former Westminster, California, deputy police chief Jeffrey Noble and Roger Clark, formerly of the Los Angeles County Sheriff's office, were authorities on the use of force. Both men wrote reports that found that the officers used poor tactics that led to the fatal shooting. The Rice family publicly released those reports. Then they asked McGinty to allow Noble and Clark to testify before the grand jury.

Clark's report said in part, "It is absolutely critical to emphasize that no weapon was visible to either Officer Loehmann or Officer Garmback upon their arrival on the scene. Officer Loehmann jumped out of the car with his gun in his hand before the car had even come close to a complete stop. Thus, it appears that Officer Loehmann must have unholstered his gun while en route to the call."[17]

In accordance with the Rice family's request, Clark, whose report concluded that the shooting was unjustified, was called to testify before the grand jury. However, Clark told *GQ* magazine in an exclusive interview, that prosecutors didn't seem very interested in hearing his point of view.

Clark told writer Sean Flynn that the prosecutors repeatedly described Tamir as an "active shooter" in front of grand jurors, though no shots were ever fired by Tamir, the gun was not real in any case, and there was no one in the park for Tamir to shoot.[18] Clark recalled that one of the prosecutors, a white man named Matthew Meyer, paced back and forth with a pellet gun like the one Tamir had in his waistband on the day he was shot dead by police. It seemed that he was using it as a prop.

Clark wanted to explain that a use-of-force incident should be viewed in context, and not just from the moment when shots were fired. He thought it mattered that the officers had sped toward Tamir and skidded to stop just a few feet away from him. Clark told *GQ* that he tried to tell the prosecutor about California case law stating that if an officer, through "tactical incompetence or outright belligerence, created the circumstance that put him in fear for his life," that should be considered.

At that point, Clark told *GQ*, Meyer wheeled on him and pointed the toy gun at his face, asking him if that would make him afraid enough to shoot. Clark told Meyer that it wouldn't scare him. But Meyer's theatrics probably scared the grand jury.

McGinty's office never confirmed Clark's account to *GQ*, because grand jury proceedings are secret and therefore can be kept from the public. But the other tactic McGinty's prosecutors evidently used to justify the killing was blaming the victim.

After the grand jury proceedings concluded, assistant prosecutor Matthew Meyer said it was "extremely difficult" to tell the difference between the pellet gun and a real one. He also repeatedly said that Tamir was big for his age. He was five feet seven and weighed close to two hundred pounds, and he wore a man's extra-large jacket and size 36 pants. Meyer claimed Tamir could have passed for someone much older, despite his lack of facial hair and his round, childlike face. And it's clear that Officer Frank Garmback, who described Tamir as "maybe 20" when he called the shooting in to radio dispatch, thought Tamir was older, as well.

That doesn't justify the officers' actions, however. It simply confirms what researchers found in a study of how some police officers view Black children.

The Essence of Innocence: Consequences of Dehumanizing Black Children was published by the American Psychological Association's *Journal of Personality and Social Psychology* just a few months before Tamir was killed. In the study, researchers found, "Black boys as young as 10 may not be viewed in the same light of childhood innocence as their white peers, but are instead more likely to be mistaken as older, be perceived as guilty and face police violence if accused of a crime."[19]

Their findings were drawn from testing 176 big-city police officers, mostly white males, whose average age was thirty-seven. The goal was to determine the officers' levels of two distinct types of bias—prejudice and unconscious dehumanization of Black people.

The participants' personnel records were utilized to determine whether they had used force while on duty. Researchers found that those who dehumanized Blacks were more likely to have used force against a Black child in custody than officers who did not dehumanize Blacks.

Researcher Phillip Atiba Goff summed up the findings this way: "Children in most societies are considered to be in a distinct group with characteristics such as innocence and the need for protection. Our research found that Black boys can be seen as responsible for their actions at an age when white boys still benefit from the assumption that children are essentially innocent."[20]

That statement reads almost like a premonition, because police and prosecutors refused to assume that twelve-year-old Tamir Rice deserved a presumption of childlike innocence. Instead, they repeatedly painted him as if he were responsible for his own death.

In truth, Tamir is dead because adult police officers who did not see him as a child recklessly took his life. Then a mostly white power structure, headed by a prosecutor whose team falsely described Tamir as an active shooter, ascribed adult attributes to a child, hired so-called experts to justify the shooting, and ultimately recommended that grand jurors choose not to indict. McGinty, in his role as prosecutor, essentially defended the police, and in doing so, engineered the officers' escape from criminal consequences.

There were numerous protests when McGinty announced there would be no indictment, including an action at Cudell Commons, near the gazebo where Officers Garmback and Loehmann pulled up in a speeding police cruiser and shot Tamir to death. One of the demonstrators was a Black man named Art Blakey. The Cleveland native told the *Los Angeles Times* he wasn't surprised by the grand jury's decision.

"There never has been any justice in these police murders," Blakey said. "We're supposed to swallow these things whole as if this is business as usual."[21]

Tamir's family refused to swallow it whole. Through their lawyers, they issued a statement conveying sadness and disappointment that the officers weren't indicted, but they also made it clear that they were not surprised. They placed the blame squarely on McGinty.

"It has been clear for months now that the Cuyahoga County Prosecutor Timothy McGinty was abusing and manipulating the grand jury process to orchestrate a vote against indictment," the statement said. "Even though video shows the police shooting Tamir in less than one second, Prosecutor McGinty hired so-called expert witnesses to try to exonerate the officers and tell the grand jury their conduct was reasonable and justified."[22]

For his part, McGinty tried to rationalize what his office had done to orchestrate non-indictments, and while doing so, he continued to blame Tamir and give the officers the benefit of the doubt.

"If we put ourselves in the victim's shoes, as prosecutors and detectives try to do, it is likely that Tamir—whose size made him look much older and who had been warned that his pellet gun might get him into trouble that day—either intended to hand it to the officers or to show them it wasn't a real gun," McGinty said. "But there was no way for the officers to know that, because they saw the events rapidly unfolding in front of them from a very different perspective."[23]

It would take years for a Cleveland City official to conclude that the true responsibility for endangering everyone involved sat firmly in the lap of Officer Frank Garmback. In May 2017, Cleveland safety director Michael McGrath gave Garmback a ten-day suspension for not alerting police radio that he and Loehmann had arrived at the park, for pulling the police cruiser just a few feet from Tamir, and for proceeding without waiting for backup.

The punishment was a slap on the wrist, but it was still too much for the police union, which appealed the suspension. Though arbitrator Daniel Zeiser agreed that Garmback "escalated the situation unnecessarily, exposed both him and Loehmann as well as Rice to unreasonable risk of harm, and precipitated the fatal shooting," Zeiser reduced Garmback's suspension to five days.[24]

In reducing the suspension, Zeiser reiterated that Garmback was not being punished for killing Tamir. He was being punished for using improper tactics.

Timothy Loehmann, the officer who shot Tamir, was also punished, though not for killing a twelve-year-old child. Instead, he was fired from the department for lying on his job application and failing to disclose that he would have been fired from the Independence Police Department if he had not been allowed to resign.

The tragic irony is that Loehmann, who was declared unfit to be an officer by the Independence Police Department after a series of incidents including dismal performance in firearm training, killed Tamir in just the kind of high-stress situation a deputy police chief said Loehmann couldn't handle.

But let's be clear. Punishing those officers should have been a matter of criminal prosecution, not internal police department discipline. Tamir's killers did not face criminal consequences because they were police officers, and prosecutor Timothy McGinty, whose job performance in gaining criminal convictions depended on police, was determined not to charge them.

McGinty was voted out as Cuyahoga County prosecutor after Black voters and their allies targeted him in the wake of his handling of the Tamir Rice case. Still, replacing him did not fix the systemic issue that can make prosecutors take sides in police-involved shootings.

A Human Rights Watch investigation found that there is a "natural conflict of interest when district attorneys—who typically work closely with the police to bring cases against suspected criminals—are faced with prosecuting those same officers."[25] Because local or state prosecutors rely on police testimony to win convictions, and frequently rely on police union endorsements to win election, they are often beholden to police and reluctant to prosecute them.

McGinty, who faced the ire of police unions after a previous attempt to prosecute a police officer, chose a different tact in the Tamir Rice case, and because of McGinty's actions, or lack thereof, neither officer faced the criminal prosecutions they should have.

Even now, Tamir Rice's family is working to get the justice they did not receive from McGinty or the federal government. In April 2021, Tamir's family asked the US Justice Department to reopen its investigation into Tamir's death, after it was closed in the last days of the Trump administration.[26] But if McGinty had vigorously pursued indictments in the first place, perhaps that wouldn't be necessary.

That's why local prosecutors who work closely with police departments must not be allowed to lead investigations of those departments. In addition, police departments must not be allowed to investigate themselves. Both scenarios represent clear conflicts of interest and are a direct threat to the lives of Black people.

THE DEMAND

Use independent prosecutors to eliminate the prosecutorial conflicts of interest that prevent the charging and imprisonment of police who unjustifiably kill. To do so, institute state-by-state legislation modeled after a 2019 New Jersey law requiring that state attorneys general, not county prosecutors, handle investigations and prosecutions for deaths by police violence. In addition, introduce automatic recusal for any prosecutor who works directly with an officer being investigated for police violence. And finally, create or bolster recall mechanisms that empower voters to immediately remove prosecutors who seek to protect abusive police officers.

8

TRAYVON MARTIN

THE CASE AGAINST STAND-YOUR-GROUND LAWS

TRACY MARTIN AND HIS SEVENTEEN-YEAR-OLD SON TRAYVON spent a lifetime bonding over sports. Since Tracy was an athlete in his own right, Trayvon often shadowed him on playgrounds and parks, watching and learning from his father.

That bond was evident on the evening of February 26, 2012, as they sat and watched the NBA All-Star Game together at an apartment in the Retreat at Twin Lakes, a gated community in Sanford, Florida. Tracy, who was divorced from Trayvon's mother, Sybrina Fulton, was staying there with his fiancée, Brandy Green, and Trayvon had been visiting with them for a week.

The game, like every NBA All-Star affair, was a mix of celebrity glitz and athletic virtuosity. R&B icon Mary J. Blige sang the national anthem, while hip-hop star Nikki Minaj performed a medley of her hits during player introductions. Ultimately, though, it was the game that stole the show, with the Oklahoma City Thunder's Kevin Durant scoring 21 points by halftime as his Western Conference team took a 19-point lead.[1]

Trayvon wanted to get some snacks before the second half, so he put on a hoodie to guard against the Florida rain and walked to a nearby 7-Eleven. There, he purchased a bag of Skittles and an Arizona iced tea, but as he walked through the gated community to get back to the townhouse and his father, a man named George Zimmerman was watching. The neighborhood watch volunteer, who identified as white and Hispanic, didn't like what he saw as he patrolled in his car, so he called the police using a non-emergency number.

"Hey, we've had some break-ins in my neighborhood," Zimmerman said, "and there's a real suspicious guy, uh, [near] Retreat View Circle, um, the best address I can give you is 111 Retreat View Circle. This guy looks like he's up to no good, or he's on drugs or something. It's raining and he's just walking around, looking about."[2]

"OK, and this guy is he white, Black, or Hispanic?" the dispatcher asked.

"He looks Black," Zimmerman said.

"Did you see what he was wearing?"

"Yeah. A dark hoodie, like a gray hoodie, and either jeans or sweatpants and white tennis shoes. He's . . . he was just staring."

"OK, he's just walking around the area," said the dispatcher.

"Looking at all the houses," Zimmerman said, later adding, "Now he's just staring at me."

After the dispatcher asked a few more questions, Zimmerman said, "Yeah, now he's coming towards me. . . . He's got his hand in his waistband. And he's a Black male."

He told the dispatcher that Trayvon looked to be in his late teens. "Something's wrong with him," he said. "Yup, he's coming to check me out, he's got something in his hands, I don't know what his deal is."

The dispatcher assured Zimmerman that police were coming.

"Okay," he said. "These assholes they always get away."

Seconds later, as Zimmerman was giving the dispatcher directions to his location, he suddenly stopped and said, "Shit, he's running."

"He's running?" the dispatcher asked. "Which way is he running?"

"Down towards the other entrance to the neighborhood . . . fucking punks."

"Are you following him?" the dispatcher asked.

"Yeah."

"OK, we don't need you to do that."

Zimmerman didn't listen, though. He followed Trayvon anyway, and at some point, he went a step further, getting out of his car to confront the unarmed teen.

Phone records show that Trayvon called his friend Rachel Jeantel around 7:10 p.m., a few minutes after Zimmerman called the police.[3]

Trayvon and Rachel, who is Black, had known each other since attending the same elementary school in Miami. But in that moment, according to testimony she later provided in open court, Rachel was on the phone listening to her childhood friend tell her that a man was watching him.

"I asked him how the man looked like," Rachel said under questioning from Sanford prosecutor Bernie de la Rionda. "He just told me the man—the man looked creepy . . . like a creepy ass [cracker]."[4]

Rachel testified that Trayvon said the man started following him and that Trayvon told her he wanted to lose him. Eventually, Rachel testified, "I just told him, run."

"And then he . . . he told me he's almost there," Rachel said in her testimony. "So as he was walking, he just complaining the man still following him and then he told me he's going to run from the back. . . . Then the phone just shut off. Then I had called back. He answered. . . .

"I asked him where he at. He told me he at the back of his daddy's fiancée house. . . . I said, you better keep running. He said, no, he lost him. . . . I could still hear him breathing hard."

Rachel testified that she was doing her hair while she was talking to Trayvon, and as she went into the bathroom and closed the door, she could hear her friend on the other end of the line. It sounded like he was having a conversation with someone else.

Rachel called Trayvon's name to try to get his attention. That's when she said she heard Trayvon ask someone, "Why are you following me for?"

Then she heard what she called "a hard breath man kind of saying, 'What you doing around here?' "

"Then I started saying, 'Trayvon, Trayvon, what's going on?' I heard a bump. I have a feeling it was the bonk of the headset. Trayvon had a headset. . . .

"Then I started hearing grass sound . . . wet grass sound. . . .

"Then I kept calling Trayvon, Trayvon. I started hearing a little bit of Trayvon saying, 'Get off, get off.'

"Then suddenly the phone hung up. Shut off. . . . And I had called him back."

Trayvon didn't answer the phone, she said.

But as the incident escalated, calls poured in to the police.

In one call, a neighbor whispered, "Hurry, please. . . . There's someone screaming outside. There's a gunshot, hurry up. . . . There's someone screaming. I just heard a gunshot."[5]

A female caller said she heard someone "screaming and hollering" for help.

In some of the calls, the screaming was audible in the background, and while it was never firmly established whether the screams came from Trayvon or Zimmerman, one fact was certain: George Zimmerman fired a single shot from his nine-millimeter semi-automatic pistol, hitting Trayvon Martin.

By the time officers arrived, Trayvon was facedown in the grass, bleeding from a single gunshot wound on the left side of his chest.

A police sergeant checked for a pulse and found none. Then, for the next six minutes, he and another officer conducted CPR. A neighbor came out with a plastic bag to seal Trayvon's wound. A few minutes later, firefighters and paramedics arrived and continued to try to revive him.

At 7:30 p.m., Trayvon was pronounced dead.

He was unarmed and carrying only a bag of Skittles, a can of Arizona iced tea, a cell phone, headphones, a lighter, and a little over forty dollars.[6]

Police questioned Zimmerman at the scene and noted that he was bleeding from the nose and the back of his head. The self-described neighborhood watch captain had a concealed carry permit for the weapon and claimed that Trayvon had attacked him, hitting him in the nose and knocking him to the pavement. He said he shot Trayvon in self-defense.

Tests of the weapon later showed evidence that Zimmerman had touched the firearm, while Trayvon had not. In addition, scrapings from beneath Trayvon's fingernails contained none of Zimmerman's DNA. Such evidence is usually present after a lengthy struggle.

After questioning Zimmerman at the scene, police took him into custody, and while Zimmerman claimed he was lightheaded as a result of his wounds, he refused a trip to the hospital and was taken to the police station, where he was questioned at length. That night, Zimmerman's wife brought a new set of clothes to the station so that Zimmerman could turn his wet and soiled clothes over as evidence.

Then, after killing an unarmed teenager he'd followed and confronted after a police dispatcher told him not to do so, George Zimmerman was allowed to go home. Trayvon's race may have influenced the Sanford Police

Department's decision not to charge Zimmerman that night, but there was another factor—one that would silently influence the views of everyone involved in the case.

Florida's stand-your-ground law, which makes it justifiable for someone to use deadly force if they believe they're in danger of being killed or seriously harmed, and to do so without having to retreat, seemed to give Zimmerman legal protection for what he'd done.

However, nothing could protect Tracy Martin from what was coming. He didn't know what had happened to his son.

The pain of that night was still fresh in Tracy's mind when I interviewed him in 2015, three years after George Zimmerman shot and killed Trayvon. Tracy also remembered the good times he'd shared with his son, and he freely shared all he could recall.

Tracy, a truck driver who grew up in the impoverished city of East St. Louis before moving to Miami in his early twenties, lit up when he talked about Trayvon. He recalled meeting Sybrina Fulton at a Christmas party—how they had dated for a year and half before they married. Sybrina cursed Tracy's name while going through the pain of childbirth, he said, but when Tracy cut the umbilical cord and heard their child yell in the nursery, Tracy knew he and Trayvon would have much in common.

"He was stubborn," Tracy told me. "And from the moment I really got to embrace him, I knew that this was a part of me that would just, kinda . . . do certain things that I did, because he wouldn't stop hollering and my mother said when I was born, I wouldn't stop hollering. So, I knew right then, this kid is gonna be like me. . . . From early on we built a friendship. We built a bond."[7]

Tracy played baseball, Trayvon played football, and the father and son spent many long days on the playing field. But after one such day, when Trayvon was nine years old, tragedy struck. Tracy and Trayvon had been on the field all day, and when they got home, they were exhausted. Trayvon was hungry, though, and he wanted to eat before they settled down to watch the Miami Hurricanes play the North Carolina Tarheels on television.

Tracy put grease in a pot on the stove to fry chicken wings, but as the grease heated up, both he and Trayvon fell asleep.

"The grease had actually been on from 9:30 at night and I woke up coughing," Tracy told me. "The grease had started spilling out over the pot and the kitchen cabinets caught on fire. My first instinct when I saw the fire . . . I took a towel and threw it over the pot, but I didn't know how heavy the towel was. The towel dragged the pot off the stove and the grease hit my legs. I had third-degree burns from my knees down to the bottom of my feet and what happened was my body instantly went in shock."

Trayvon dragged his father to safety that night. Then, when the ambulance came and the paramedics told Trayvon he couldn't ride with them, the boy displayed the stubbornness Tracy knew. "He was like, 'No, I'm riding in the ambulance with my dad,'" Tracy recalled. "This is the personality that I know he had in him that I had in me."

Trayvon's personality was grounded not just in genetics, but in a determination to win that was nurtured on the playing fields of South Florida.

"In Miami we have an atmosphere," Tracy told me. "When you play sports, sports don't really see Black, brown, white, or yellow. He was raised on the park with a lot of Latin kids, a lot of Jewish kids, a lot of white kids."

But ultimately, the young man who played defensive end and wide receiver on a youth football team, who dragged his father to safety after a grease fire, and who grew up around kids of every race and ethnicity, was profiled by someone who believed a Black boy in a hoodie looked suspicious.

Trayvon, like any seventeen-year-old boy, was not perfect. He'd recently been suspended after school officials found a bag containing traces of marijuana in his backpack, but Trayvon had no criminal record, and his father said he wasn't a bad kid by any stretch of the imagination.

That's why, on the night Trayvon was shot, Tracy knew that his son would've come back from the store if he could have, so at four in the morning, Tracy called the police. Then he filed a missing person's report.

"They ended up calling me back about six thirty in the morning, and they told me they were going to send a patrol unit out to the house," Tracy told me. "It hadn't dawned on me that something was wrong. I'm thinking the unit's coming out to get more information about him being missing. So it was three cars pulled up. The first car was a community service car, the second car was a uniformed officer's car, and the third car was an undercover car.

"So, they get out. They introduce themselves, and it didn't dawn on me that the first person to introduce himself to me was the—he was sort of like the chaplain for the police department. And he introduced himself as—he said, 'I'm the chaplain of the Sanford Police Department.' And then the detective came up. He introduced himself. He said he was with the Major Crimes Unit. And it's not registering.

"So, he asked me did I have a picture of Trayvon. I told him, 'Yeah I had a picture.' I had just taken a picture of him and two more of my kids playing around two days before. So I showed him the picture and he told me I'll be right back. And it was drizzling outside. He asked if I minded if we went in the house.

"He asked me when was the last time I seen Trayvon and what did he have on and he went through the formalities, and then he said, 'I'm going to show you a picture. You tell me if this is your son.' And he pulled out a picture, and it was him on the ground dead."

In the days after the shooting, with police dragging their feet on charging Zimmerman, Tracy Martin retained two Black, Florida-based attorneys—Benjamin Crump and Natalie Jackson. On March 8, Tracy, along with fiancée Brandy Green, a cousin, and the attorneys, held a press conference demanding that the police file murder charges against Zimmerman.

At that press conference, attorneys Crump and Jackson pointed out that Zimmerman had no reason to follow Trayvon and even less reason to confront him. Once he called police, Zimmerman should have allowed officers to handle the situation, the lawyers said, rather than patrolling the neighborhood with a gun as if he were a police officer.

As pressure mounted for answers in the case, Sanford police chief Bill Lee, who is white, told reporters that his department was in the midst of a "thorough and fair" investigation of the incident, and that they'd found nothing to refute Zimmerman's claim that he shot Trayvon in self-defense.

"Until we can establish probable cause to dispute that," Lee said, "we don't have the grounds to arrest him."[8]

Many thought Lee was hesitant to charge Zimmerman because of Florida's stand-your-ground law, which gives anyone who feels a reasonable threat of death or bodily injury the right to "meet force with force, including deadly force," and to do so without having to retreat.[9]

Promoted by the National Rifle Association, the law passed in Florida in 2005 and was later pushed in numerous states by a corporate-backed, limited government group called the American Legislative Exchange Council (ALEC). In the racially charged atmosphere surrounding Trayvon's death, Black people and their allies saw stand your ground as an impediment to justice, while Zimmerman's mainly white supporters saw the law as justification for Zimmerman's decision to kill an unarmed teenager.

However, Florida representative Dennis Baxley, who sponsored the law in 2005, told reporters that the law does not allow people to "pursue and confront," as Zimmerman admittedly did by following Trayvon and getting out of his car to question him.[10]

As the controversy around the case grew, Trayvon's parents, Tracy Martin and Sybrina Fulton, created a Change.org petition demanding Zimmerman's arrest. The DOJ sent representatives to Sanford both to investigate and to address mounting community tensions.

Events snowballed after that. George Zimmerman's father, Robert Zimmerman, wrote a letter to the *Orlando Sentinel* saying the media's portrayal of his son as a white racist was "extremely misleading." The letter read, in part:

> George is a Spanish speaking minority with many black family members and friends. He would be the last to discriminate for any reason whatsoever. . . . The media portrayal of George as a racist could not be further from the truth. . . .
>
> At no time did George follow or confront Mr. Martin. When the true details of the event become public, and I hope that will be soon, everyone should be outraged by the treatment of George Zimmerman in the media.[11]

Of course, some of Robert Zimmerman's claims were simply wrong. First, George Zimmerman's father is white and his mother is Hispanic, making George Zimmerman a white Hispanic, and not just a Spanish-speaking minority. Second, George Zimmerman did follow Trayvon, which he admitted to the dispatcher in his recorded call to the police. Third, George Zimmerman got out of his car before police arrived and got close enough to Trayvon for a physical confrontation to take place.

But Zimmerman's father wasn't the only one talking about the case. Even the National Sheriffs' Association (NSA), which runs Neighborhood Watch programs across the nation, weighed in on the accusations against Zimmerman.

"The alleged action of a 'self-appointed neighborhood watchman' last month in Sanford, FL significantly contradicts the principles of the Neighborhood Watch Program," NSA executive director Aaron D. Kennard, a retired sheriff, said in a press statement. "NSA has no information indicating the community where the incident occurred has ever even registered with the NSA Neighborhood Watch program."[12]

As the Sanford Police Department completed its investigation and handed its findings over to the Office of the State Attorney, Sanford police chief Bill Lee temporarily stepped down amid criticism of the department's handling of the case. Florida governor Rick Scott appointed state attorney Angela Corey as a special prosecutor, and on March 23, as the Change.org petition reached one million signatures, President Barack Obama weighed in on the case.

"I can only imagine what these parents are going through," he said, speaking from the Rose Garden. "And I think every parent in America should be able to understand why it is absolutely imperative that we investigate every aspect of this, and that everybody pulls together—federal, state, and local—to figure out exactly how this tragedy happened."[13]

Then Obama said something that has stuck with me, and with most Black parents who heard his words that day. "If I had a son, he'd look like Trayvon. When I think about this boy, I think about my own kids."

I do too. That's what makes the needless death of Trayvon Martin so heartbreaking, and the failure to get justice so infuriating.

On April 11, 2012, Florida state attorney Angela Corey announced that Zimmerman was being charged with second-degree murder in the shooting death of Trayvon Martin. Zimmerman turned himself in and was jailed, but lawyers who looked at the charge wondered how long he would remain behind bars. To win a conviction on second-degree murder, prosecutors would need to prove that Zimmerman intentionally pursued Trayvon instead of shooting him in self-defense, that he acted with hatred or ill will, and that the stand-your-ground law did not apply.

It was a difficult legal argument to win, but special prosecutor Angela Corey said she was confident her team could prevail.

Even before the trial, there was legal maneuvering involving lawyers and judges, all of whom were white. Zimmerman's lawyer, Mark O'Mara, requested that Judge Jessica Recksiedler step aside from presiding over the case due to potential conflicts of interest, since Recksiedler's husband's law partner was under contract to do on-air analysis of the case for CNN. Recksiedler was subsequently replaced by Seminole County Circuit Court judge Kenneth Lester.

On April 20, Judge Lester oversaw Zimmerman's first bail hearing. There, Trayvon's parents saw Zimmerman for the first time, face to face, and when the handcuffed and shackled killer took the stand in the Sanford, Florida, courtroom, he addressed them directly.

"I wanted to say I am sorry for the loss of your son," Zimmerman said to Tracy Martin and Sybrina Fulton, who were seated in the second row. "I did not know how old he was. I thought he was a little bit younger than I am. And I did not know if he was armed or not."[14]

Trayvon's parents didn't respond, but during the two-hour hearing, there were tough questions from both sides.

Zimmerman's attorney, Mark O'Mara, asked a white state investigator if he knew who started the fight between Trayvon and Zimmerman.

The investigator, Dale Gilbreath, said no.

Not to be outdone, assistant state attorney Bernardo de la Rionda asked Zimmerman about the five separate statements he gave to police. "Do you agree you changed your story?" the prosecutor asked.

"Absolutely not," Zimmerman said.

At the end of the two-hour hearing, with Zimmerman claiming indigence, Judge Lester did what some believed was unthinkable. He set Zimmerman's bail at $150,000 and released him with several restrictions, including an electronic ankle bracelet to monitor his movements.

Ten days later, Zimmerman waived his right to a pre-trial immunity hearing where he could have tried to have the case dismissed under a provision of the stand-your-ground law. Winning at such a hearing would mean he could not be charged in criminal court or sued in civil court for killing Trayvon, but winning would not have been easy.

At a pre-trial immunity hearing, the defendant—not the prosecutor—bears the burden of proof. In addition, providing testimony at such a hearing gives the prosecutor a preview of how the defense plans to argue the case. Bearing all that in mind, Zimmerman's team decided to take their chances at trial.

However, court strategy wasn't the only thing Zimmerman had to consider. There was also the matter of paying for his defense. To do so, Zimmerman had launched a website with a PayPal link just shortly before he was charged, quickly raising about $200,000. While he was jailed, Zimmerman and his wife, Shellie, hid the money from the court, even going so far as to speak about the cash in code during recorded phone calls. They also used veiled language to talk about a second passport that Zimmerman had locked away in a safe-deposit box.

After his lies were discovered, Zimmerman was once again taken into custody on June 3, but five weeks later, he was granted another bail hearing. In a new order setting Zimmerman's bail at $1 million, Judge Lester blasted Zimmerman's deception, pointing out that giving false or misleading information in a bail application—which is a felony—could result in future contempt proceedings.

The judge also wrote that "under any definition, the defendant has flouted the system" and "tried to manipulate the system when he has been presented the opportunity to do so."[15]

"It is entirely reasonable for this court to find that, but for the requirement that he be placed on electronic monitoring, the defendant and his wife would have fled the United States with at least $130,000 of other people's money," the judge wrote, adding that the court had "thwarted" Zimmerman's attempt to flee.

A few days later, Zimmerman's attorneys claimed that Judge Lester used "gratuitous, disparaging" language about Zimmerman in his order and said Zimmerman had "a reasonable, well-founded fear that he [would] not receive a fair trial by this court."[16]

An appeals court agreed with them, and Lester was forced to step down for telling the truth about a killer who'd lied to the court about his assets, secured a second passport under false pretenses, and appeared to be a flight risk.

A year later, when the trial began, Zimmerman was on his third judge, and for those seeking justice for Trayvon, things only seemed to get worse.

The lawyers argued everything from the jury's composition to the instructions the jurors would receive from the judge. At the end of those arguments, the six-person jury included five white women, one Hispanic woman, and no Black people. Embedded in the instructions that a white judge named Debra Nelson read to the jury were words that came directly from the stand-your-ground statute.

"If George Zimmerman was not engaged in an unlawful activity and was attacked in any place he had a right to be," Judge Nelson told the jurors, "he had no duty to retreat and had the right to stand his ground and meet force with force, including deadly force if he reasonably believed that it was necessary to do so to prevent death or great bodily harm to himself or another or to prevent the commission of a forcible felony."[17]

On the heels of the judge's instructions, assistant state attorney John Guy began his opening statement by raising the other issue driving the case—race.

Guy hammered home the idea that in a community that had experienced several recent burglaries, Zimmerman assumed that Trayvon was one of the people involved in that criminal activity, and he did so because Trayvon was Black.

"'Fucking punks. These assholes, they always get away.' They were the words in this grown man's mouth as he followed in the dark a 17-year-old boy he didn't know," Guy, a white man, told the jury.[18]

He continued,

> Excuse my language, but they were his words, not mine. Those were the words in that man's chest when he got out the car armed with a 9mm semi-automatic pistol to follow on foot Trayvon Benjamin Martin, who was walking home armed with twenty-three ounces of Arizona brand fruit juice and a small bag of Skittles candies.
>
> As the smoke and the smell of that fatal gunshot rose in a rainy Sanford night, Trayvon Martin, 21 days removed from his 16th year, was face down in the grass, laboring through his final breaths on this Earth.

Zimmerman's defense team never raised the stand-your-ground law during the trial, but because it was included in the jury instructions, the controversial law was always there, reminding jurors that if Zimmerman feared for his life, he could meet force with force, and he had no duty to retreat.

The defense claimed that Zimmerman acted in self-defense after Trayvon ambushed and attacked him, punching him in the nose and banging his head against the concrete. To bolster their narrative that Trayvon was the aggressor, the defense had Zimmerman's parents testify that it was their son screaming for help in the background of a neighbor's 911 call.

The prosecution, meanwhile, relied heavily on the testimony of Trayvon's friend, Rachel Jeantel, who was on the phone with Trayvon as Zimmerman followed him on the night he was killed.

Through frustration, mumbled answers, and constant interruption from both the prosecution and the defense, Rachel's testimony was difficult to follow, and that seemed to hurt the prosecution's case. But the overall arc of her story was clear. Zimmerman followed Trayvon, who was frightened of Zimmerman and wanted to get away from him. Then, after Zimmerman got out of his car and the two were face-to-face, Zimmerman asked Trayvon what he was doing in the neighborhood, and Trayvon asked why Zimmerman was following him. Soon after, there was an altercation—sounds of a falling headset and steps on wet grass. After that, Trayvon never answered his phone again.

Zimmerman didn't testify in the trial. Instead, prosecutors played the taped statements he'd given to police. But in his closing argument, assistant state attorney Bernie de la Rionda said Zimmerman was a liar.

De la Rionda pointed out that in his five interviews with police, Zimmerman made numerous statements that defied reason. He claimed that Trayvon grabbed for his gun, though Trayvon's DNA was not found on the weapon. He claimed Trayvon slammed his head against concrete twenty-five times, though he only had a couple of cuts. He claimed he was afraid of Trayvon, though he got out of his car to follow him. He claimed that Trayvon was punching him and covering his mouth, all while reaching for his gun, which Trayvon would have needed three hands to do.

Ultimately, none of that swayed the jury. Zimmerman was found not guilty, and according to at least one of the six jurors, the stand-your-ground law played a major role in the decision.

The woman, known only as Juror B-37, told CNN's Anderson Cooper that "because of the heat of the moment and the 'stand your ground,' he had a right to defend himself. If he felt threatened that his life was going to be taken away from him or he was going to have bodily harm, he had a right."[19]

Ultimately, the juror said, they had no choice but to acquit.

Therein lies the problem. Stand-your-ground laws not only give murderers the legal justification to kill others. These laws also signal to jurors that killers have a right to take lives under the vague notion that they feel threatened.

This kind of legal sleight of hand, which allows perceived threats to be viewed as real, jeopardizes the lives of Black people, and, according to recent research, it particularly endangers Black men.

In a 2017 study, researchers found that people see Black men and boys as larger and more threatening than their similarly sized white counterparts.[20] They sometimes use those stereotypes to justify using violence against Black males, and Trayvon Martin was no exception.

Black men are not the only ones facing a more dangerous world with stand-your-ground laws. Black women are too, and in the wake of Zimmerman's acquittal, it was three Black women—Alicia Garza, Opal Tometi, and Patrisse Cullors—who created the #BlackLivesMatter hashtag, which has since grown into an international movement to protect all Black lives, including those in the LGBTQ community.

However, as the movement has grown, so has the threat of stand-your-ground laws. As of 2020, legislation similar to Florida's has been adopted by twenty-seven states with the help of two powerful forces—the National Rifle Association and the American Legislative Exchange Council.

"ALEC seized on the Florida law, which became part of ALEC's 'model legislation' portfolio," writes Rukmani Bhatia of the Center for American Progress. "The result was widespread efforts for state legislatures across the nation to enact these laws."[21]

The results have been devastating for Black people.

In November 2012, when a white man named Michael Dunn claimed he was threatened after confronting a group of Black teenagers over loud music in a Jacksonville, Florida, gas station, he fired into their car, killing seventeen-year-old Jordan Davis while claiming self-defense. Dunn was eventually convicted.

In February 2020, when Gregory and Travis McMichael, both white, confronted a twenty-five-year-old unarmed Black jogger named Ahmaud Arberry, they initially avoided arrest by claiming they were standing their ground and acting in self-defense. The McMichaels, along with William "Roddie" Bryan, a third white man who filmed the encounter, are awaiting trial after being charged with Arberry's murder.

"These tragic deaths are not outliers," writes Bhatia. "Researchers at American University found that approximately 30 people die each month in a 'stand your ground'-related incident in states with these laws enacted.

Data show that states with a version of 'stand your ground' laws see increased rates of homicides and injuries related to gun violence."[22]

Behavioral scientist Andrew Morral and economist Rosanna Smart, writing for the RAND Corporation blog, reviewed available research on stand-your-ground laws and arrived at similar conclusions. Their review found "'moderate' evidence—the second strongest level of evidence—that these laws are associated with an increase in homicides. Since publication of RAND's report, at least four additional studies meeting RAND's standards of rigor have reinforced the finding that 'stand your ground' laws increase homicides. None of them found that 'stand your ground' laws prevent violent crime. No rigorous study has yet determined whether 'stand your ground' laws promote legitimate acts of self-defense."[23]

Then, of course, there is the racism. John Roman, of the Urban Institute's Justice Policy Center, analyzed data from the FBI's Supplemental Homicide Report for 2005–2009 in states with stand-your-ground laws. "The odds that a white-on-black homicide is ruled to have been justified is more than 11 times the odds a black-on-white shooting is ruled justified," Roman told Bloomberg News. "No dataset will ever be sufficient to prove that race alone explains these disparities. But there are disparities in whether homicides are ruled to be self-defense, and race is clearly an important part of the story."[24]

It is indeed, which is why, in the interest of Black people's survival, stand-your-ground laws must be challenged in courts, overturned in legislatures, and ultimately erased from the books.

If there is any doubt that these laws are meant to target Blacks, one need only examine a November 2020 proposal made by Florida governor Ron DeSantis. The governor, a white conservative, proposed an update to Florida's stand-your-ground law in the wake of a summer of protests seeking racial justice after George Floyd and others were murdered by white police officers.

In an effort that seems to target the very Black Lives Matter protests that began with the killing of Trayvon Martin, DeSantis's proposal would update the law to justify lethal force in instances of looting, criminal mischief, and arson "that results in the interruption or impairment of a business operation."[25]

DeSantis called the proposal "anti-mob" legislation. But neither De-

Santis nor other conservatives proposed similar edicts after a largely white mob attacked the US Capitol in an attempt to overturn an election, killing a police officer and causing four other deaths in the process.

Thus, we must call stand-your-ground laws what they are: anti-Black laws. We must fight them with every fiber of our being.

THE DEMAND

Eliminate stand-your-ground laws, which have served to justify the murders of Black and brown people, beginning with Trayvon Martin. These laws, which expand the definition of self-defense to a level that endangers all citizens, and especially people of color, have been shown to increase homicides rather than prevent them. Therefore, they must face legal challenges until they are wiped from the books at the state level and prohibited by federal law.

9

DEBORAH DANNER

THE CASE FOR DEFUNDING THE POLICE

ON TUESDAY, OCTOBER 18, 2016, JAYQUAN BROWN, A BLACK security guard at a Bronx apartment building, was among those who called police to report that one of the residents was acting erratically.

Deborah Danner, a sixty-six-year-old Black woman who'd been diagnosed with paranoid schizophrenia, was in the midst of a mental health crisis that night. She tore posters off the wall and screamed so loudly in the hallway outside her seventh-floor apartment that she was audible in the background when Brown dialed 911.

That wasn't the first time Deborah's mental illness prompted neighbors and security to call law enforcement. Police in the Forty-Third Precinct were familiar with Deborah because they'd responded twice before to her outbursts at the apartment building on Pugsley Avenue. In the other two incidents, police were there to help emergency medical technicians take Deborah to a psychiatric ward. This time, things went differently.

Four police officers and two emergency medical technicians arrived first, Brown said. Later, thirty-one-year-old police sergeant Hugh Barry, who is white, arrived with another officer and Jennifer Danner, Deborah's sister.

There are slight differences in the various accounts of what happened after that, but everyone who was there agrees on two things. Five minutes after Sergeant Barry arrived, Deborah Danner was dead from two gunshot wounds, and Barry, the senior officer on the scene, fired the shots.

Within six hours, Barry was stripped of his gun and badge and placed on modified duty. New York mayor Bill de Blasio and police commissioner James O'Neill said Barry did not follow established NYPD protocols for dealing with emotionally disturbed people. Bronx borough president Ruben Diaz Jr., who is Latino, and city council speaker Melissa Mark-Viverito, who is white, called for state investigations.

In the days and weeks that followed, activists marched, media swarmed, and a city that was supposed to be implementing better officer training to deal with the mentally ill was once again in the eye of a storm.

Bronx district attorney Darcel Clark, who is Black, asked the state to impanel a special grand jury in the case. As state attorney general, Eric Schneiderman had the power to investigate the police shooting of a civilian under a 2015 executive order signed by Governor Andrew Cuomo—an order that was put in place after a grand jury declined to indict then officer Daniel Pantaleo for killing Eric Garner. Schneiderman, who is white, declined to open a state investigation into Deborah's case, saying the evidence indicated that Deborah had a weapon when she was shot and killed by Sergeant Barry.

Clark, the Bronx DA, was not deterred. As a former judge, she'd seen one side of the criminal system, and as the wife of a New York City police detective, she'd seen the other. In Deborah Danner's case, Clark saw injustice, so she impaneled a grand jury and secured an indictment against Barry. The eight-year police veteran was charged with second-degree murder, first- and second-degree manslaughter, and criminally negligent homicide.

The trial took place in 2018, nearly a year and a half after Deborah Danner was killed. It was then that the story of what happened in Deborah's seventh-floor apartment began to take shape. It came out in the testimony of those who were involved.

Jayquan Brown, the Black security guard who was among those who called police that evening, said Deborah's screams reverberated in the halls when he was on the phone with police.

For about fifteen to twenty minutes, Brown said, the police and emergency medical technicians talked to Deborah, trying to convince her to drop the scissors she was holding so they could take her to the hospital.

Deborah insisted that she didn't need help from the police or from the EMTs, Brown said. She wanted them to back off.

"You could hear Deborah screaming and yelling, 'F you! Die! Leave me alone!'" Brown said in his testimony. "She was slamming her cabinet doors, screaming."[1]

Though an emergency medical technician said in her testimony that

Deborah had already put down the scissors before Sergeant Barry arrived, Barry told the court a different story.

The police sergeant testified that when he arrived at 6:22 p.m., Deborah was sitting on her bed angrily cutting up paper with the scissors. He testified that he tried to convince her to come out of her bedroom and talk to an emergency medical technician, but she profanely refused while holding up the scissors like a knife.

Barry said that he tried again to convince Deborah to talk with the medics and that she agreed to let them come into the bedroom to talk to her. He said he told her they couldn't come in if she had the scissors. Then, according to Barry's testimony, Deborah slammed the scissors down on her nightstand, went to her bedroom door, and said, "This is as far as I'm going."[2]

Barry testified that he didn't believe he would be able to talk Deborah out, so he nodded to the other officers to indicate that he was about to rush the woman. As he tried to grab her, Barry said, Deborah ran back into the bedroom.

"She was much faster than I thought," Barry told the court.

But, as prosecutor Newton Mendys said on the trial's opening day, Barry "made a bad situation worse. He created a situation that was rushed, hurried, careless, reckless, chaotic and ultimately tragic."[3]

Barry claimed that once Deborah made it back into the bedroom and he went in after her, he saw her sitting on the bed holding a baseball bat she'd taken from beneath the sheets. He testified that Deborah, who was sixty-six years old, was nimble enough to jump up on a bed from a sitting position, take on a batter's stance, and shift her weight forward to swing at him—all before he could do anything but fire his service weapon.

Barry, who is six feet tall and weighed 225 pounds at the time of the incident, claimed that a woman more than twice his age, who was five feet six and overweight, made him fear for his life, a claim that is hard to believe. And yet, that is the story he told.

Barry testified that when Deborah tried to use the bat, he couldn't retreat because the other officers were crowded behind him, and he couldn't use his Taser, which was also in his reach, because it was "not appropriate" against a bat.

"She was in the middle of a swing," Barry said, "and that's when I shot her."[4]

Jayquan Brown, in his testimony, recalled that moment. He said he heard a "rumble, a tussle," followed by two quick shots.

"Jennifer Danner tried to run down the hall," Brown told the court. "I physically grabbed her. She was frantic." He said he remembered her screaming, " 'Oh my God, they shot my sister!' "[5]

Except there was no "they." Sergeant Barry was the only one to pull his gun, and the only one to shoot. When he did so, he was the only one in the bedroom with Deborah, and so he acted alone. Only one of the other officers on the scene, Camilo Rosario, said he saw the shooting take place. Rosario told the court that Deborah was swinging the bat when Barry shot her.

However, under cross-examination by prosecutor Wanda Perez-Maldonado, it was revealed that Barry did not follow department protocols for dealing with emotionally disturbed people. Not only did he not use his Taser, as Mayor de Blasio and Commissioner O'Neill had confirmed earlier, but Barry had also left a shield and restraining straps for dealing with disturbed people in his car.

When the prosecutor suggested that Barry could have waited Deborah out instead of rushing to try to subdue her, Barry said he thought she might retrieve the scissors and hurt someone.

"In situations like this," Barry testified, "sometimes you have a split second. You can't always make a plan."[6]

Perhaps in another circumstance that might be true, but there is a special unit within the NYPD that regular officers can call for help with mentally ill people. It's called the Emergency Service Unit, and it is staffed with officers who are specially trained to employ de-escalation techniques in such situations.

At the time Barry shot Deborah, the NYPD was also providing crisis intervention training to its 36,000 officers. Only 4,400 officers had participated in the four-day training at the time. Barry was not among them.

Therein lies the problem. The NYPD had known for decades that officers needed specialized training to deal with the mentally ill. More than three decades later, only a fraction of the department's officers had received such training. This, despite the fact that in 2016 the NYPD estimated that it dealt with more than a hundred thousand calls about emotionally disturbed people each year.[7]

Learning to better deal with the mentally ill was not a priority, and those who mishandled such situations were rarely punished.

Barry was found not guilty on all charges after killing Deborah Danner, and while the city of New York paid $2 million to the family to settle a wrongful death lawsuit, the family did not see that as justice.

Perhaps worse, Deborah's family is not alone.

Mental illness, like every issue in America, is impacted by the dynamics of race. As of 2017, Black adults in the United States were more likely than their white counterparts to report persistent symptoms of emotional distress, like sadness and hopelessness, according to the US Department of Health and Human Services Office of Minority Health.[8] Yet Blacks face ongoing disparities when it comes to accessing mental health care services.

In a 2017 report, the American Psychiatric Association noted that Black people "often receive poorer quality of [mental health] care and lack access to culturally competent care." Perhaps most troubling, "only one-in-three African Americans who need mental health care receives it."[9]

The barriers that create such disparities are many. They include a lack of health insurance, a scarcity of culturally competent mental health care providers, and a dearth of Black providers in the mental health field. Having access to Black providers is important, since many Blacks distrust the medical industry. That suspicion is well earned because of past racist medical atrocities like the Tuskegee experiments, in which Black men with syphilis did not receive proper treatment for their illness so doctors could document their symptoms as the disease progressed.

But in a community where mental strength is required just to deal with the daily indignities of racism, mental illness is sometimes seen as a weakness. That stigma leaves many who are in need of help afraid to ask for it. With so many barriers to quality care, Black people experiencing mental health crises are too often left to the police, and the results have been disastrous for many, including those in the LGBTQ community.

Kawaski Trawick, a thirty-two-year-old Black gay man from the Bronx, was experiencing what neighbors and advocates called "emotional distress" when he called the fire department in April 2019 to help him get into his locked apartment. According to footage of the incident from the building's security cameras, Kawaski, who had a history of substance abuse and other mental health issues, was walking up and down the hallway in his underwear and a jacket when firefighters responded and forced the door open. Kawaski walked inside.

A few minutes later, two NYPD officers arrived and pushed the door open.

"Why are you in my home?" Kawaski asked, standing near his stove with a bread knife in one hand, according to body cam footage.

The officers didn't answer his question. Instead, Herbert Davis, a Black officer with sixteen years of experience, spoke calmly to Kawaski, asking him to put down the knife. The other officer, Brenden Thomas, who is white, was more forceful, telling Kawaski to drop the knife. In less than two minutes, Officer Thomas had pulled his Taser and his gun.

Kawaski was muttering to himself, when, without warning, Officer Thomas deployed his Taser. Then, as the officers entered the apartment and tried to handcuff him, Kawaski yelled, "Get away!" before rushing toward them and yelling, "Get out, bitch!"

As Davis told his partner not to shoot, Thomas shot four times, hitting Kawaski twice. He died that night from his injuries. The whole interaction took just 112 seconds.

Charles Lieberman, a retired NYPD detective and expert on handling people in crisis, told Pro Publica that the officers escalated the situation "by opening the door without permission or authorization of the resident, when the resident expressed that they were not wanted and without any other criminal behavior being observed."[10]

Bronx District Attorney Darcel Clark did not pursue charges against the officers. But the fact that Kawaski Trawick was killed by police as he experienced a mental health episode is not unusual. Studies say it's more common than we know.

In 2015, the Treatment Advocacy Center published a widely cited study suggesting that those with untreated mental illness who are involved in a police incident are sixteen times more likely to be killed by the police than others who are stopped by law enforcement.[11]

"It should horrify but not surprise us that people with untreated mental illness are overrepresented in deadly encounters with law enforcement," study coauthor John Snook said in a statement released with the study. "Individuals with untreated mental illness are vastly overrepresented in every corner of the criminal justice system. Until we reform the public policies that have abandoned them there, these tragic outcomes will continue."[12]

He's right.

The *Washington Post*, whose Fatal Force database has tracked every police killing since 2015, found that 23 percent of those killed by police in the last six years were mentally ill.[13] Yet for those who are experiencing mental health crises, the police are still called on to act as first responders. At worst, this results in fatalities, but in the normal course of things, it results in arrests.

According to the National Alliance on Mental Illness, people who are experiencing a mental health crisis are more likely to encounter police than to get the medical help they need. That leads to nearly two million people with mental illness being booked into jails each year.[14]

Most are not violent criminals. In fact, the vast majority of them are awaiting trial and have not been convicted of any crime. But if jailing those who are mentally ill is not the goal, what is the alternative?

William G. Brooks III, chief of the Norwood, Massachusetts, police department, touts a curriculum called Mental Health First Aid for Public Safety as a solution.

He describes the program as an

> actionable public safety training program that gives police officers a simple, effective way to intervene during any mental health crisis, from an immediate crisis that endangers the public or the officer to non-crisis situations, like approaching someone who is exhibiting symptoms of a mental illness or overdose.
>
> It equips every officer with the necessary skills to recognize the symptoms of mental illnesses and substance use, engage the person in crisis, de-escalate the incident and connect the person to needed care.[15]

But even when officers are trained to help those with mental health issues, are police better equipped to do so than medical professionals? More importantly, should serving the mentally ill be left to law enforcement when mental illness is not a crime?

Remarkably, Deborah Danner herself had written an essay in which she explored that very question. She wrote,

> We are all aware of the all too frequent news stories about the mentally ill who come up against law enforcement instead of mental health professionals and end up dead. We should all be aware that these circumstances represent very, very serious problems that need addressing. Baldly stated, some of these problems are:
>
> Teaching law enforcement how to deal with the mentally ill in crisis so

> as to prevent another "Gompers" incident. Many years ago, here in NY, a very large woman named Gompers was killed by police by shotgun because she was perceived as a "threat to the safety" of several grown men who were also police officers. They used deadly force to subdue her because they were not trained sufficiently in how to engage the mentally ill in crisis. This was not an isolated incident.[16]

Deborah was referring to Eleanor Bumpurs, an elderly Black woman who, like Deborah, was mentally ill, and resided in the Bronx.

In October 1984, Eleanor, who lived alone in a fourth-floor apartment in a public housing complex called the Sedgwick Houses, fell behind by four payments on her $98.65 monthly rent.[17]

The New York City Housing Authority initially sent city marshals to serve an eviction notice, but Eleanor, who was experiencing a mental health crisis, screamed threats through the door. That's when authorities called the police.

The department's elite Emergency Service Unit responded, sending a group of white officers to storm Eleanor's apartment. Inside they found the 260-pound woman armed with a ten-inch knife. What happened next is told entirely from the perspective of police, because Eleanor didn't live to share her side of the story.

Police claimed that one of the officers tried to restrain Eleanor with a special Y-shaped pole. Two others moved toward her with plastic shields while trying to pin her hand against the wall so she couldn't harm them with the knife.

Police said that Eleanor swiped at them with the knife, knocking the pole aside. Then, according to police, she went after one of the officers.

At that point, Officer Stephen Sullivan, who was standing behind the other officers, fired his 12-gauge single-barrel shotgun, striking Eleanor in the hand. Then he fired again, striking her in the chest and killing her.

Like Deborah Danner, Eleanor Bumpurs was sixty-six years old when she was shot and killed in her apartment by a white police officer, and just as they were in Deborah's case, New York's Black community was outraged. So were others who knew that what had happened to Eleanor Bumpurs was wrong.

Mario Merola, a white man who was the Bronx district attorney at the time, impaneled a grand jury, and Sullivan was indicted on a charge of second-degree manslaughter. Merola said the fact that Sullivan fired two shots was important, since the manslaughter charge required someone to recklessly cause the death of another person.

The police commissioner, Benjamin Ward, said that Sullivan had complied with departmental guidelines that were in place at the time of the shooting. Nevertheless, he suspended the officer without pay after he was indicted.

Merola, asked to respond to the commissioner's assertion that Sullivan had followed the rules, said, "Hitler's people also followed guidelines. You can't just follow orders blindly and escape your individual responsibility."

However, Merola did not put the blame entirely on the officer. He also blamed New York City's Human Resources Administration for not providing Eleanor Bumpurs with the psychiatric help and welfare assistance that would have stopped the eviction from going forward in the first place.

Merola also questioned the police officer's story about what actually happened in Eleanor's apartment, saying that "it was anatomically impossible" for Eleanor to have held on to a knife after being shot in the hand.

The doctor who treated Eleanor Bumpurs in the emergency room after the shooting agreed. Harold Osborn, the doctor in charge when Eleanor arrived at Lincoln Hospital, told the *New York Times* that there was "overwhelming medical evidence" that she'd been shot twice.

"My professional opinion is that she was shot first in the hand and totally disarmed and rendered helpless, and that she was then shot a second time in the chest," Dr. Osborn said in an interview.

In the end, none of that mattered. Sullivan was tried and acquitted in 1987 for killing Eleanor Bumpurs, a mentally ill Black woman, in an incident that took place because she couldn't pay her back rent of less than four hundred dollars.

However, the case was so controversial that it forced changes in the way the New York Police Department handled those who were struggling with mental illness. The new guidelines required patrol officers to wait until a supervisor arrived before confronting someone who was emotionally disturbed. The department's Patrol Guide was rewritten to require officers to isolate suspects in mental distress and to establish "a zone of safety" around them.

Yet even with those changes and the subsequent introduction of Crisis Intervention Training to the officers of the NYPD, Deborah Danner, who had written about her illness and about the murder of Eleanor Bumpers, was killed in a strikingly similar scenario more than thirty years after Eleanor Bumpurs was shot dead.

Perhaps, if the problem was isolated to New York City, the solution would be a matter of changing local policy. Unfortunately, that's not the case.

In Philadelphia in 2020, a Black man named Walter Wallace, who was carrying a small knife while experiencing a mental health crisis, was shot dead by two officers after police were called to the family home for the third time in a day. In Rochester, New York, a handcuffed and naked Daniel Prude, who was also Black and in the midst of a mental health crisis, suffocated after police put a spit hood on his head and pinned him to the ground. A grand jury later declined to file charges against the officers in the Prude case.

There are many more cases in cities and towns across America, but here's the point: Protecting the mentally ill who are in crisis situations is not just about training local police officers to better deal with them. It is also about employing mental health professionals who are not police officers. It is about reallocating funding in ways that provide real assistance. It is about recognizing that this problem springs from policy decisions that stretch back for decades.

In the report *Innovative Solutions to Address the Mental Health Crisis: Shifting Away from Police as First Responders*, researchers Stuart Butler and Nehath Sheriff of the Brookings Institution point out that handling mental health crises falls to police because of America's "longstanding, inadequate level of mental health services" fueled by a decades-long decline in the number of inpatient psychiatric beds.[18]

"The police become the responders of last resort, and the jails become the mental hospitals of last resort," criminologist Peter Scharf, of the Louisiana State University School of Public Health and Justice, told *USA Today*. "Increasingly, the police and correctional system become the last option."[19]

However, there are alternatives to using traditional law enforcement to deal with mental health issues. One of them, according to Brookings, is the Crisis Intervention Team. "These teams are comprised of specially trained police officers and mental health professionals," the researchers write. "They collaborate to address and de-escalate high-stress mental health situations, while having the range of skills required to handle possibly dangerous developments. The teams can also help individuals obtain longer-term care."[20]

In Anne Arundel County, Maryland, for example, the Crisis Intervention Unit uses mobile crisis teams that "include two clinicians: one an independently licensed mental health professional, and the other a masters level clinician. The team responds to a police radio call and is a valuable tool for patrol officers who have options other than making an arrest," according to Brookings.

The county system also includes a phone line to funnel nonemergency calls to trained staff who can provide direct assistance or refer callers to other resources. In addition, Anne Arundel County trains its police officers in mental health first aid. Since that training began, according to county officials, police use of force there has dropped by 21 percent.

However, Anne Arundel County, with a median household income of more than twice the national average, has resources that other places simply don't. They can provide multiple hours of training and recruit master's level clinicians and independently licensed mental health professionals as volunteers. That's rarely possible in Black and brown communities. That's why, in places like the Bronx, where Deborah and Eleanor were shot, and West Philadelphia, where Walter Wallace was shot, police are the primary responders to mental health crises.

It's now clear that the paradigm must change. If affluent communities have access to the kinds of resources that safely serve the mentally ill while decreasing the number of use-of-force incidents, other communities should have those resources too. And if the money for those services is not currently available, it should be reallocated from the budgets that are currently reserved for police.

This is not to say that police should completely disappear. But in situations where no laws are being broken, or when medical help is required, or when society and the individual need healing rather than punishment, the police should not be deployed.

It's clear that when police are asked to resolve problems they aren't qualified to handle, they can escalate conflict instead of calming it. There are low-cost solutions that can serve to eliminate such risk, and they are now being implemented in places one might never expect to see them.

■ ■ ■

Alexandria, Kentucky, is a town of nearly ten thousand just south of Cincinnati, Ohio. With a population that is 98.6 percent white, it is a place where policing functions differently than it does in diverse northern cities like New York or Philadelphia.[21] Race is less of a factor in daily police interactions in Alexandria because Blacks simply don't live there.

Still, the town deals with many of the other social ills that affect most communities, and police are expected to address them. In 2016, non-crime-related issues made up two-thirds of the calls to police in Alexandria, and then police chief Mike Ward wanted to try a different approach.[22]

In a story chronicled in *The Guardian*, Ward said his officers were repeatedly called to the same homes to deal with ongoing problems police couldn't permanently resolve. Many of the calls were rooted in issues created by substance abuse, domestic conflict, or mental health issues.

The calls had one thing in common, however. They weren't best suited to be handled by police, so Ward decided to do something unusual. He convinced the city to hire a social worker connected to the police department. Doing so cost half as much as hiring and equipping a new police officer, so it made sense from a budgetary standpoint, and if it worked, it would free up officers from repeated calls regarding noncriminal issues.

The strategy was fairly simple. Police in Alexandria continued to act as first responders to whatever calls they received. If the call did not concern law enforcement, the non-uniformed social worker would then follow up. Typically, the social worker connected residents with needed help on issues like mental illness, substance abuse, homelessness, and domestic conflicts. And when family conflicts morphed into domestic abuse, the social worker acted as a victim advocate.

Though Alexandria's police officers initially scoffed at the idea, thinking it would take needed resources from law enforcement, the program's effectiveness quieted the doubters. In fact, it worked so well that by 2020, Alexandria had two social workers assisting the police instead of just one.

But while the successful use of social workers in an all-white environment can serve as a model, it doesn't indicate how the strategy would work when race is at the center of conflict. The cruel reality is that Black and brown people are treated differently not just by police but also by some of the social workers and medical professionals who would be called on to assist with social or mental health crises.

We'll learn more about how social workers help augment police responses in communities of color when they are hired to assist police in Louisville, a larger and more diverse Kentucky city. Bringing social workers to Louisville is one of many reforms that were promised after police lied to gain a no-knock warrant, killed Breonna Taylor in a botched drug raid, and escaped criminal liability in a secret grand jury proceeding that prompted calls for Kentucky attorney general Daniel Cameron's impeachment.

It's ironic, really. In a racially just system, a Black emergency medical technician like Breonna Taylor might very well be the type of person called to help mentally ill Black women like Deborah Danner or Eleanor Bumpurs. Instead, all three of them are dead at the hands of white police officers. That's not a coincidence, and it is why race must always be part of the conversation in the push to reallocate funding from law enforcement to medical and social services. Just as importantly, the discussion can't happen in a vacuum. It must be part of a larger conversation on police reform.

That's what's happening in Connecticut, where in 2020, Governor Ned Lamont signed a police accountability bill that included a number of new provisions. It included changes to qualified immunity that would hold police personally liable for wantonly violating a citizen's rights, for intervening and reporting abusive behavior by colleagues, and for not finding a reasonable alternative to deadly force. Within that bill was a section calling for the study of the utilization of social workers by police departments.

The National Association of Social Workers, Connecticut Chapter (NASW/CT), in its written testimony before the state's Police Transparency and Accountability Task Force in October 2020, offered support for the idea and laid out why social workers were qualified to engage in such an effort, noting,

> Social workers have extensive training in working with diverse populations, are problem solvers, experts in de-escalation, and through a "person-in-environment" approach assist individuals and families to resolve societal problems. Social workers are aware of community resources and know how to access them. Social workers are advocates for clients in a way that creates trust and supportive relationships. These are the types of skills that make for successful engagement within the community. Just as police officers are experts in addressing issues of law enforcement, social workers are experts in resolving social problems that bring individuals into encounters with the police. Formal and informal connections between police and social workers is a recipe for improved outcomes for certain 911 calls.[23]

According to the testimony from NASW/CT, social workers are also being used to assist police in other areas of the country. "In Denton, Texas, four licensed clinical social workers are employed for direct service, overseen by a social work supervisor," the organization wrote. "This has created a unified special mental health unit within the police department."

In addition, the testimony notes, "Dallas, Texas has instituted the Right Care program where police officers respond to assure the scene is secure and clinicians immediately follow. The Right Care clinical team handles 200–250 calls per month. In those city districts where Right Care is operating there has been a ten percent reduction in citations for disorderly conduct, intoxication and trespassing."

Their testimony also noted a program called CAHOOTS, an acronym for Crisis Assistance Helping Out on the Streets, which was started in 1989 by White Bird Clinic as a community policing initiative. In 2019, crisis workers from the program handled 24,000 calls, and only 150 required police backup.[24]

Police are also turning to social workers in Olympia, Washington, where a crisis response unit is staffed by two social workers. In Denver, Colorado, the police department's Support Team Assisted Response (STAR) sends a two-person civilian team consisting of a paramedic and a social worker on calls involving substance abuse and mental health. In Albuquerque, New Mexico, the city created a separate community safety department staffed by mental health and health care professionals.

Sometimes, though, tragedy becomes the impetus for change. That's what happened in Buffalo, New York, where the police shot a mentally ill homeless Black man named Willie Henley after he allegedly hit an officer with a bat.

Protesters flooded the streets following the shooting, which Henley survived, and officials subsequently suggested the creation of a new program that would pair social workers with police officers on calls dealing with mental illness. Not everyone in Buffalo supported it, however. A group of social workers from Western New York Agents of Change told reporters from Buffalo's NPR-affiliate that police and social workers do things differently, and they might not work well together.[25]

In some cases, that could very well be true, which is why there should be options other than traditional social work for handling community conflicts, especially when harm has been done. One such approach is restorative justice. In his book *Defund Fear: Safety Without Policing, Prisons, and Punishment*, Zach Norris explains: "Restorative justice places the needs of the survivor at the center. It avoids terms like 'victim,' 'perpetrator,' and 'offender,' because of the way in which those labels stick to a person forever and deny them the ability to evolve, to heal and to change."[26]

Instead, restorative interventions involve dialogue run by trained facilitators who help those who've done harm take responsibility and those who've been harmed to be made whole through a series of actions including apology, reparation, and consequences.

Given that police in far too many instances have suffered no consequences for the harm they've done to the mentally ill and other vulnerable people in Black communities, I believe it's time for us to take up their refrain. We fear for our lives.

For that reason, we call for a portion of our tax dollars to be stripped from the police budget and reallocated to life-sustaining systems staffed by trained professionals who value our lives as much as we do.

THE DEMAND

Move one-third of police funding to pay for trained social workers, mental health professionals, and conflict resolution specialists. Acknowledge that racist policies have left Black communities without the mental health facilities necessary to treat our most vulnerable, and deliver restorative justice to those who've been harmed as a result. Doing so will not only protect our most vulnerable citizens from being victimized by violent policing in the future. It will also allow officers to address the crime we pay them to reduce.

10

SANDRA BLAND

THE CASE FOR ENDING RACIAL PROFILING

THE FIRST TIME I HEARD GENEVA REED-VEAL SPEAK OF HER late daughter, she did so with the passion of a preacher. Her voice rose and fell with righteous indignation and when she paused, I was anxious to hear more.

Sandra Bland's mother is a force to be reckoned with, and when I interviewed her for my radio program in 2016, she told me that her daughter was too. Sandra had shown as much while asserting her rights during her traffic stop arrest, and even through the pain of recalling what it was like to see that, Geneva made room for pride:

> As a mom I will tell you, to watch that tape, 'cause I saw the tape the same time everybody else did; I was so proud of her in that moment, because she was letting that officer know, "No sir, no, no no—I know my rights. You're not just gonna pull me up out of this car, but I'm gonna get out, because I will wait to see you in court." And as she got out, she was still taping. So, when you talk about a mother viewing her radical daughter who said, "No, I'm not taking this," . . . [I felt] very proud of her. . . . And I will be championing for Sandy all of the rest of my days. The world will never forget her.[1]

Indeed, we will not, because Sandra's mother is a truth teller. There are no euphemisms. No feeble attempts to soft-pedal her beliefs. What happened to her daughter is simple, in her view. Authorities in Waller, Texas, lied about Sandra's arrest, lied about monitoring her in detention, and lied about how Sandra died.

Clearly, someone was going to pay a price for that, and if anyone could tilt the scales of justice in her daughter's favor, it was Geneva Reed-Veal.

First, though, we would have to know the Sandra who lived before the hashtag. We would have to see beyond the chaos that defined her final days.

At twenty-eight, Sandra was searching for her purpose. A supporter of the Black Lives Matter movement who posted videos on police brutality and racial strife, Sandra wanted to fix what was wrong in the world. Much like other Black content creators who dare to speak up for Black lives, she was relentlessly trolled by racists. One person asked her if she was trying to use race to incite people rather than unite them. She posted a video in response.

"Honestly, I feel that my goal is to racially unite," Sandra said in the video, which she filmed in her car in April 2015. "In the process of doing that, some people will be racially incited, [or] upset."[2]

Those who found her videos upsetting had the option not to watch, she said. But for white people who wanted to "get past" America's history of racism, Sandra had a simple answer. First, they would have to acknowledge the hard truths of America's racist past. Then they would have to admit that racism and white privilege persists in the present. She used policing as an example, and said that white people have a different relationship with police officers than Blacks do. For whites, she said, "the police don't even suspect you of doing anything wrong, and that's just how it is."

Like so many of us, Sandra had seen the reality of race and policing in America. Drivers of color, and Black people in particular, were racially profiled by white officers who disproportionately stopped them for traffic infractions in attempts to investigate other crimes. Then there were the videos—those terrible and violent viral snippets of Black people being killed by white police officers.

One such video emerged just days before Sandra called for racial unity. In it, Walter Scott was shot in the back by Officer Michael Slager in South Carolina. The year before, a teen named Laquan McDonald was shot sixteen times by Officer Jason Van Dyke in Sandra's hometown of Chicago. That same year, Tamir Rice was shot in Cleveland, Michael Brown was shot in Ferguson, Eric Garner was choked in New York, and Ezell Ford was shot three times, once in the back, in Los Angeles.

Sandra was living through all of it in real time, and as she sought to find ways to make a difference in the lives of Black victims of brutality and discrimination, she was also trying to find a personal sense of purpose.

That's what she talked to her mother about during a trip to visit relatives in Tennessee. At least one of her goals was beginning to come into focus for her, and she shared it with her mother when they returned to Chicago.

"Mom, my purpose—I know what my purpose is," Geneva recalled her daughter saying. "My purpose is to go back to the South and stop all the injustices against Blacks in the South."[3]

For Sandra, that meant returning to her alma mater, Prairie View A&M, and taking a job as a student ambassador. She had already talked about it a lot, Geneva said, so when the school called on a Tuesday and asked her to interview for the job, Sandra stepped out on faith, packed everything she owned into her car, and drove to Texas.

By Thursday, after doing the interview, Sandra got the job, her mother said. She was well on her way to fulfilling the purpose they'd talked about. Then on Friday, Sandra called her mother and told her she was leaving the school to drive to Walmart.

"She said, 'Mom I'll call you back when I get out of Walmart,'" Geneva said. "Well, of course that call never came because Sandy was pulled over at about 4:30 in the afternoon on a Friday. She was minding her own business. Officer Brian Encinia profiles her . . . U-turns the car, speeds up on her. So, she's thinking, 'Okay, this guy is in a hurry.' She gets over without using her traffic signal. I do it all the time. There are a million people across the world who do it all the time. And she had no idea he was going to be pulling her over."

The interaction between Sandra and Texas state trooper Encinia, who is white, began with Encinia greeting her, identifying himself, and telling Sandra that he pulled her over because she changed lanes without signaling. "What's wrong?" he asked her. "How long have you been in Texas?"[4]

"Got here just today," Sandra said.

"Okay. Do you have a driver's license?"

Sandra handed it to him and he asked where she was headed. Then he went back to his car and returned a few minutes later.

"Okay ma'am," he said. "You okay?"

"I'm waiting on you. This is your job. I'm waiting on you. When are you going to let me go?"

"I don't know," Encinia said, and for the third time, he mentioned that Sandra looked like something was wrong. "You seem very really irritated."

"I am," Sandra said. "I really am. I feel like it's crap what I'm getting a ticket for. I was getting out of your way. You were speeding up, tailing me, so I move over and you stop me. So yeah, I am a little irritated, but that doesn't stop you from giving me a ticket, so [give me the] ticket."

"Are you done?"

"You asked me what was wrong," Sandra said. "Now I told you."

"Okay."

"So now I'm done, yeah."

Encinia then made an odd request—one that had nothing to do with the car stop. "You mind putting out your cigarette, please? If you don't mind?"

"I'm in my car, why do I have to put out my cigarette?" Sandra asked.

"Well, you can step on out now."

"I don't have to step out of my car."

"Step out of the car."

"Why am I . . ."

"Step out of the car!"

"No, you don't have the right," Sandra said. "No, you don't have the right."

"Step out of the car."

"You do not have the right. You do not have the right to do this."

"I do have the right. Now step out or I will remove you."

"I refuse to talk to you other than to identify myself," Sandra said, as Encinia talked over her. "I am getting removed for a failure to signal?"

"Step out or I will remove you," the trooper said. "I'm giving you a lawful order. Get out of the car now or I'm going to remove you."

"And I'm calling my lawyer," Sandra said.

"I'm going to yank you out of here," Encinia said, reaching inside the car.

"Okay, you're going to yank me out of my car? Okay, alright."

As Encinia called for backup, Sandra said, "Let's do this."

"Yeah, we're going to," Encinia said as he tried to grab her.

"Don't touch me!" Sandra said.

"Get out of the car!"

"Don't touch me. Don't touch me! I'm not under arrest—you don't have the right to take me out of the car."

"You are under arrest!"

"I'm under arrest? For what? For what? For what?"

Encinia got back on the radio and called for backup once again. Then he yelled at Sandra. "Get out of the car! Get out of the car now!"

Sandra repeatedly asked him why she was being arrested, and as Encinia yelled and threatened to drag her from the car, she questioned him once again.

"I will light you up!" Encinia yelled, drawing his stun gun and pointing it at Sandra, who was taping the interaction on her phone.

"Wow," Sandra said as she exited the car. "Wow."

As Encinia repeatedly yelled at her, Sandra was in disbelief. "For a failure to signal?" she said. "You're doing all of this for a failure to signal?"

As Encinia told her to get over on the side of the road, Sandra continued to record the interaction.

"Get off the phone!" Encinia yelled repeatedly, and when Sandra explained that she had a right to record what was happening, he shouted, "Put your phone down!"

Sandra slammed the phone down on the trunk of her car, and as Encinia directed her to stand on the sidewalk, she began to question him.

"You feelin' good about yourself? For a failure to signal? You feel real good about yourself, don't you? You feel good about yourself, don't you?"

"Turn around," Encinia said. "Turn around. Turn around now. Put your hands behind your back."

"Why am I being arrested?"

"Turn around . . ."

"Why can't you . . ."

"I'm giving you a lawful order," he said. "I will tell you."

But Encinia didn't tell her and instead repeatedly claimed that he was giving her a lawful order. As he placed her in handcuffs, Sandra told him why she believed he wouldn't answer.

" 'Cause you know this straight bullshit," she said. "And you're full of shit. Full of straight shit. That's all y'all are, is some straight scared cops. South Carolina got y'all bitch asses scared. That's all it is. Fucking scared of a female."

"If you would've just listened," Encinia said.

"I was trying to sign the fucking ticket—whatever."

Encinia told her to stop moving, and Sandra said, "Oh I can't wait 'til we go to court. Ooh I can't wait. I cannot wait 'til we go to court. I can't wait. Oh I can't wait! You want me to sit down now?"

"No."

"Or are you going to throw me to the floor? That would make you feel better about yourself?"

"Knock it off!" Encinia shouted.

"Nah that would make you feel better about yourself," Sandra said. "That would make you feel real good, wouldn't it? Pussy ass. Fucking pussy. For a failure to signal you're doing all of this. In little ass Prairie View, Texas. My God they must have . . ."

"You were getting a warning, until now you're going to jail."

"I'm getting a—for what? For what?"

As Encinia jerked Sandra by the handcuffs she complained that he was about to break her wrists. He asked her if she had anything illegal on her person. She told him no. Officer Penny Goodie, a Black female officer from the Prairie View Police Department, arrived to back up Encinia. Both officers claimed Sandra was resisting. Then things got worse.

"Get on the ground!" Encinia yelled.

"For a traffic signal!" Sandra shouted.

"You are yanking around, when you pull away from me, you're resisting arrest."

"Don't it make you feel real good, don't it? A female for a traffic ticket. Don't it make you feel good, Officer Encinia? You're a real man now. You just slammed me, knocked my head into the ground. I got epilepsy, you motherfucker."

"Good," Encinia said. "Good."

As Encinia tried to convince a bystander to leave, Sandra thanked that person for taping what they'd seen. When a paramedic and another officer arrived, Encinia claimed that Sandra kicked him, an accusation he would use as justification for arresting her on a felony charge of assaulting a public servant.

As Sandra, now in handcuffs, was placed in another officer's car, Encinia called a supervisor to explain what had happened. Encinia's side of the conversation was recorded by his dashcam video.

"I tried to de-escalate her," Encinia said. "It wasn't getting anywhere, at all. I mean I tried to put the Taser away. I tried talking to her and calming her down, and that was not working."

Encinia went on to explain that he stopped Sandra for failing to signal a lane change, but he didn't tell the supervisor that he ordered Sandra out of her vehicle after she asked why she had to extinguish her cigarette. Encinia also made another key statement while talking to the supervisor.

"When I had her down on the ground and the other officer came," he said, "I told her stop resisting and that's when I told her you're under arrest."

Except Encinia told Sandra she was under arrest before she even exited the vehicle, which calls into question why he told her to get out of the car in the first place. Encinia's explanation, which he would later document on a sworn probable cause affidavit, was that he ordered Sandra to exit the vehicle "to further conduct a safe traffic investigation."[5]

But if Encinia was concerned about his safety during the car stop, there are a number of standard procedures he should've followed. These include using his car's public address system to instruct Sandra to lower the vehicle's windows, waiting for backup to arrive before approaching the vehicle, and checking the trunk to make sure it was securely closed. Moreover, if safety was an issue, he should not have reached into the vehicle, as he did during the stop.

A grand jury would later examine Encinia's claim that he ordered Sandra out of the vehicle to conduct a safe car stop and determine that his statement was a lie. Unfortunately, their decision came much too late for Sandra.

She was transported to the Waller County Jail on the afternoon of July 10. She would not leave that jail alive.

According to the Bureau of Justice Statistics, 1,092 inmates died in local jails in 2015. A deeper dive into the data shows that suicides accounted for nearly a third of deaths in local jails from 2000 to 2016 and that white inmates are more likely to have died in jail than Black or Hispanic inmates.[6]

"The mortality rate for white jail inmates in 2016 (240 deaths per 100,000 white inmates) was more than double the rate for black inmates

(118 deaths per 100,000 black inmates) and almost triple the rate for Hispanic inmates (87 deaths per 100,000 Hispanic inmates)," according to the report from the Bureau of Justice Statistics.[7]

Still, Black people are more likely to end up in local jails than their white counterparts. ABC News analyzed 800 jurisdictions across the country and found that between 2015 and 2018, Black people were arrested at a rate five times higher than white people. The numbers are based on an analysis of FBI data, which found that in 250 jurisdictions the disparity was even worse, with Blacks being ten times more likely to be arrested than whites.[8]

Kristen Clarke, president and executive director of the National Lawyers' Committee for Civil Rights Under Law, told ABC News that the disparities are due to overpolicing. "When we see data that shows that African Americans are singled out, unfairly targeted, disproportionately subject to arrest and prosecution—that should sound an alarm," she said.[9]

In many cases, that unfair targeting does sound an alarm, but only after tragedy strikes, as it did in the case of Sandra Bland. Stopped under questionable circumstances by an officer who claimed Sandra injured him during an arrest, Sandra was booked into the Waller County Jail, where she was asked a series of questions for a fifteen-page jail booking screening form.

That form, filled out at 5:32 p.m. on the day of Sandra's arrest by deputy jailer Oscar Prudente, included several questions related to suicide and depression. Among them: "Have you ever been very depressed?" The answer was yes. "Do you feel this way now?" The answer was yes. "Have you had thoughts of killing yourself in the last year?" The answer was yes. "Are you thinking about killing yourself today?" This time, the answer was no. "Have you ever attempted suicide? If yes . . . When? Why? How?" The answer was yes. Prudente wrote that Sandra told him she tried to commit suicide using pills in 2014 after losing a baby. Finally, Prudente asked, "Have you experienced a recent loss?" Sandra told Prudente she'd experienced loss with the death of her godmother the year before.[10]

Guards in the Waller County Jail did not put Sandra on suicide watch, despite the answers Prudente filled in while interviewing Sandra. If they had done so, the standard in place at the time would have mandated a cell check every thirty minutes. Waller County sheriff R. Glenn Smith later told the *New York Times* that the jailers decided not to put Sandra on suicide watch because she told them she was not suicidal at the time. She was just angry that she had been detained.

Prudente did not complete the booking process because he had other duties to attend to, according to an investigation by the Texas Rangers. A second booking form was filled out at 8:15 p.m. by jailer Elsa Magnus based on another interview with Sandra. This second form indicated that Sandra was taking Keppra, an anti-epilepsy medication. It also noted an alleged prior suicide attempt, but it said Sandra had never been depressed and was not experiencing depression at the time. Waller County district attorney Elton Mathis told the *New York Times* that the discrepancies between the two forms were the result of Sandra giving different answers, but Sandra's family and friends never believed she was depressed or suicidal.

LaVaughn Mosley, a longtime friend and mentor, spoke to Sandra the night she was arrested. "She was great," Mosley told the *New York Times*. "Looking forward to getting out and moving forward." Given her upbeat attitude when he talked to her, Mosley didn't believe the news that came from the jail three days later. "She was a tough girl and a strong girl," he said.[11] Suicide simply didn't make sense.

But in later testimony given to the Texas Rangers in a state investigation, Dormic Smith, one of the jailers, said Sandra wasn't eating her food and repeatedly asked to use the phone at the booking desk. On Saturday, Judge Dolores Hargrave set her bond at $5,000.[12]

It would take just $515 to get her out of jail, and Sandra was desperately trying to raise the money. Her predicament, like that of so many Black people caught in the criminal justice system, was not just racial. It was also economic.

According to the *Houston Chronicle*, Sandra called a local bail bondsman and offered her car title as collateral for him to put up the bond. The bondsman declined to do so. She also called her older sister, Shante Needham, and told her she was jailed and needed financial help to get out. The family was in the process of trying to raise the money as Sandra placed more calls to her friend LaVaughn Mosley.

Time magazine reported that by the time Mosley discovered two missed calls and a voicemail from Sandra, it was too late.

"Hey, this is me," Sandra said in the voicemail to Mosley. "I'm, um—I just was able to see the judge. I don't really know. They got me held at a $5,000 bond. I'm, I'm still just at a loss for words, honestly, about this whole process. How this switching lanes with no signal turned into all of this, I don't know. Um, but I'm still here, so I guess call me back when you can. Bye."[13]

Smith, the jailer, told investigators that after she left the voicemail for her friend, Sandra "was 'upset pretty bad' and was crying." According to the report, Sandra "talked about the arrest and told . . . Smith how she was placed on the ground, bumped her head, and was threatened with a taser."[14]

Still, Smith didn't believe Sandra was thinking about taking her own life. According to the Texas Rangers report, "Jailer Smith stated Bland told him that she had changed her life and drove from Chicago, Illinois for a job. He never once thought she was suicidal, but she appeared to be in a state of disbelief about what was happening to her."

Things came to a head on July 13. Sandra allegedly refused breakfast at 6:30 a.m. At 7:17 a.m., jailers Rafael Zuniga and Michael Serges checked Sandra's cell. Sometime after that, Sandra requested to make a call from her cell, though no call was made.

Jailers Zuniga and Serges falsified a jail log to indicate that they did an in-person check of Sandra's cell at 8:01 a.m. In actuality, according to depositions they later submitted, the log was filled out in advance, and Serges signed it at the beginning of their shift. The Texas Rangers reviewed video footage and found that no jailer physically checked on Sandra's cell at 8:01 a.m., but the Waller County Sheriff's Office later claimed the check was done by intercom.

At the time, the Texas Commission on Jail Standards mandated that all inmate cells be checked hourly and in person. Instead, two hours passed between in-person checks of Sandra's cell. Deputy jailer Cynthia Whidden told the Texas Rangers that she discovered Sandra hanging from a noose fashioned out of a plastic trash can liner at 8:59 a.m., when Whidden and jailer Rafael Zuniga went to see if the female inmates wanted recreation time.

Deputy Randy Lewis told Texas Rangers he was in the patrol room writing a report when he received a report that an inmate was hanging in the jail. Deputy Lewis and Lt. Justin Lane went to check Sandra's cell, while Deputy Henderson stayed behind at the main door to the jail so he could let EMS in when they arrived. Lieutenant Sherry Rochen, the supervisor on the scene, checked for a pulse and found none.

According to the Texas Rangers' report,

> Deputy Lewis entered the cell and he observed a female inmate on the floor and on her back with her arms outstretched. Lieutenant Sherry Rochen was performing chest compressions and he asked if she needed to be relieved. Deputy Lewis attempted mouth to mouth breathing with a protective CPR mask which covered Bland's nose and mouth. Deputy Lewis stated air would not go in and Bland's lungs did not rise. Deputy Lewis put the mask down and took over chest compressions from Lieutenant Rochen. Deputy Lewis witnessed EMS put monitors and defibrillation pads on Bland and he continued chest compressions until he was told to stop by EMS. Deputy Lewis assisted EMS [to] take their equipment out of the cell and then he left and went back to the patrol room.

At 9:06 a.m., Sandra was pronounced dead, and when Geneva Reed-Veal got the news, she was devastated.

"To receive a call like that when you know that you just talked to your baby," she said a year later as she spoke about her daughter in Philadelphia, "you know that your baby just got the dream job she talked about. But to get that type of call—to have to go to Texas, fly my baby back in a capsule under the bottom of a plane with luggage on top of her—if you think I'm shutting up you're crazy. I'm not shutting up, and the entire world will hear her story."[15]

Less than a month after Sandra's death, her mother filed a federal wrongful death lawsuit against state trooper Brian Encinia, the Texas Department of Public Safety, the Waller County Sheriff's Office, and jailers Elsa Magnus and Oscar Prudente.

The suit said that Encinia made up a reason to arrest Sandra, setting in motion the events that led to her death. The suit also placed blame on Waller County Jail personnel, who were required to monitor Sandra on a regular basis, keep her safe from injury and death, and evaluate the mental status of those who were held in custody. The suit alleges the jail failed in its responsibility to adequately monitor Sandra, failed to respond appropriately when she refused to eat, and failed to respond when she "had bouts of uncontrollable crying" while in custody.

The suit also accused Magnus and Prudente of showing a "willful, wanton, and reckless" disregard for Sandra's safety and failing to keep her safe while in custody. It also alleged that "Waller County Jail personnel were inadequately trained on the procedures for recognition, supervision, documentation, and handling of inmates who are mentally disabled, and/or potentially suicidal," in violation of Texas law.[16]

But while the lawsuit spoke of Sandra's mental state, the jailers' response when she refused to eat, and her emotional outbursts, the family was adamant about one thing. They did not believe that Sandra committed suicide. In fact, at a Chicago press conference shortly after Sandra died, their attorney said even more.

"The family of Sandra Bland is confident that she was killed and did not commit suicide," lawyer Cannon Lambert said in a statement. "The family has retained counsel to investigate Sandy's death."[17]

Later, when an autopsy report signed by Sara N. Doyle of the Harris County Institute of Forensic Sciences listed the cause of death as hanging and the manner of death as suicide, the family demanded an independent autopsy, and protesters demanded justice.

As demonstrators took to the streets, conspiracy theories began to spread. Proponents of one theory believed that Sandra was already dead in her booking photo, theorizing that she was actually lying on her back in the picture rather than standing against a wall.

To refute that rumor, officials released footage of Sandra being booked and photographed. That made little difference, because there was much more about the official response that created an air of suspicion: The failure to adequately monitor Sandra after jailers claimed she told them about a previous suicide attempt. The two different versions of her booking form. The fact that she was placed alone in a cell with a bag that could be used to harm herself. Then, just two months after Sandra's death, two of her jailers, Rafael Zuniga and Michael Serges, were quietly moved from the Waller County Sheriff's Office to the smaller Waller Police Department, even after admitting under oath that they falsified a jail log to indicate that they'd checked Sandra's cell on the day she died when they had not.

The evidence gathered by the Texas Rangers and the autopsy reports indicate that Sandra committed suicide, but even if that is true, the jailers are culpable due to their extreme negligence. But the person who is most responsible for her death is Brian Encinia, the man who made the arrest.

Encinia, who was placed on desk duty pending the outcome of the investigation into Sandra's death, told the Texas Department of Safety's Office of Inspector General, "My safety was in jeopardy at more than one time" during his interaction with Sandra. Based on videos of the arrest, that did not appear to be true, just as it wasn't true that Encinia "had Bland exit the vehicle to further conduct a safe traffic investigation," as he wrote in a sworn affidavit.[18]

In spite of all the irregularities surrounding Sandra's death, no one was indicted when a grand jury was impaneled to investigate.

That result was no surprise to those who had seen grand juries decline to indict when Darren Wilson killed Michael Brown, and when Blane Salamoni killed Alton Sterling, and when Daniel Pantaleo killed Eric Garner, and when Timothy Loehmann killed Tamir Rice. Grand juries are too often a tool for prosecutors who are seeking to avoid charging police officers. And sometimes, as it was with Breonna Taylor, a grand jury can be used to charge an officer with something that mocks true justice.

After an outcry from activists and others around the non-indictment of the jailers and others in Sandra's death, special prosecutor Darrell Jackson reconvened the grand jury. As a result, trooper Brian Encinia was indicted on a misdemeanor charge of perjury for lying about the reason he pulled Sandra from her car.

"In the probable-cause statement, Encinia stated that he had pulled her out of the car to continue the investigation. The grand jury did not believe that," special prosecutor Darrell Jordan told *The Atlantic*.[19]

If convicted of that charge, Encinia would have faced up to a year in jail and a $4,000 fine. Encinia did not go to trial, however. He was ultimately fired and agreed not to pursue another job in law enforcement in exchange for the perjury charge being dropped.

Meanwhile, the federal wrongful death lawsuit filed by Geneva Reed-Veal in the death of her daughter, Sandra, was settled. The family was paid $1.9 million,[20] and various reforms were supposed to be put in place in Waller County jails.

The county promised to provide an on-duty nurse or EMT for all shifts, to use automated sensors to ensure accurate and timely cell checks, to provide additional jailer training on booking and intake screening, and to seek passage of legislation to fund that training. The judge in the case supported the notion of naming the legislation for Sandra Bland.

The nonmonetary elements of the settlement were meant to keep other inmates from dying under similar circumstances. It didn't work.

Four years after Sandra died in custody after arguing with a white police officer, Evan Lyndell Parker, a Black man, was found hanging in his cell in the Waller County Jail after Parker was accused of killing Harry Parnell, the white, sixty-four-year-old father of a police officer.

Like Sandra's death, Parker's hanging was ruled a suicide. While the racial implications and connections to police will always raise questions about both deaths, Sandra's case was the one that was supposed to bring change, because she should never have been arrested in the first place.

In the wake of the national outrage that followed Sandra's death, there was renewed discussion of racial profiling. The practice, in which police stop Black and brown drivers for minor traffic infractions while searching for evidence of other crimes, was widely believed to be a factor in the initial car stop that led to Sandra's arrest.

Trooper Encinia found no illegal contraband during the stop, and that wasn't unusual. As author and researcher David Harris documents in his book *Profiles in Injustice*, in jurisdictions using racial targeting, police find contraband more often when they stop and search whites than when they search Blacks or Latinos.[21]

That's why, when the House Committee on County Affairs held hearings on SB-1849, also known as the Sandra Bland Act, members addressed that very issue, and found "significant racial disparities in how the Texas Department of Public Safety treats Blacks when compared to Whites after they have been pulled over for a traffic violation. The Committee also found that the way the [Department of Public Safety] records and presents the data needs to be improved."[22]

The Sandra Bland Act was meant to address these problems by strengthening Texas's anti-racial profiling law, and in its original form, the bill did just that. In addition to providing training and mental health resources for

Texas jails, it addressed racial profiling by banning pretext or "investigative" stops, which the bill's author, a Black state representative named Garnet Coleman, described as the vehicular equivalent of stop and frisk. It also required law enforcement to collect data on those stops to document racial and ethnic disparities. The bill included components to prevent people from being jailed for Class C misdemeanors that typically are punished by fines and also featured language ensuring that offenders without prior violent convictions could be released on personal bonds.

The backlash was immediate, and it came from police unions, the same groups that typically protect bad police officers at the expense of public safety. Charley Wilkison, who is white, is the executive director of the Combined Law Enforcement Associations of Texas. Wilkison said the legislation amounted to a "witch hunt" on law enforcement and claimed that changes to laws on racial profiling weren't needed, since similar laws were already on the books.[23] Republicans in the Texas legislature joined with law enforcement groups to oppose the bill, and soon after, the provisions challenging racial profiling and other law enforcement practices were systematically removed from the legislation.

In its final form, the bill focused mainly on police training and access to mental health care. "What the bill does in its current state renders Sandy invisible," Sandra's older sister, Sharon Cooper, told the Associated Press in May 2017. "It's frustrating and gut-wrenching."[24]

That didn't matter to Texas politicians. The stripped-down version of the bill was signed into law by Texas governor Greg Abbott, a white man, a month later.

That's not good enough. The same racial profiling practices that allowed Sandra Bland to be stopped, dragged from her car, and ultimately jailed for a minor traffic violation are utilized far too often in America. And make no mistake, the same racial animus that drives these practices are at the root of the way that policing plays out in too many Black communities. It is the foundation of what amounts to an attack on Black lives.

In life, Sandra Bland believed her purpose was to fight for justice for Blacks in the South. However, her purpose is bigger than that now. It is about more than Texas legislators reintroducing the original legislation that bears her name. It is about more than one community repairing its local jail. Sandra Bland's legacy must be about creating protections for the vulnerable in every county and in every jurisdiction. It must be about creating protections for those who are vulnerable to racialized policing.

For Tamir Rice and Deborah Danner, for Eric Garner and Michael Brown, for George Floyd, Breonna Taylor, Hassan Bennett, Alton Sterling, Trayvon Martin, and yes, even for herself, Sandra Bland's legacy must be about change. To secure the racial unity Sandra talked about in the days before she died, we must create a criminal justice system that treats all Americans with dignity. Doing so requires more than simply denouncing racial inequity. It requires a national push to root out racism once and for all.

THE DEMAND

Eradicate the national scourge of racial profiling by creating a federal Sandra Bland Act. Borrowing from the original intent of the Texas legislation, this new federal law must ban pretext or "investigative" stops based on race. It must create a national database that traces racial and ethnic disparities in police stops. Moreover, it must create protections that keep the indigent from being jailed for minor traffic violations, and it must create a national standard for the protections afforded to inmates in local jails.

EPILOGUE

THE STORIES IN THIS BOOK ATTACKED MY EMOTIONS IN ways I didn't know they could. I was angry while writing about the murder of George Floyd, whose journey through the perils of poverty and addiction were much like my own. His was a life seasoned with love and with dreams of basketball stardom, poisoned by run-ins with a racist criminal justice system, and punctuated by a violent death at the hands of those who should have protected him.

I mourned for George Floyd, knowing that the only difference between him and me is that I am here to tell our stories. That is the triumph of this book. A book that made me cry when I saw the impish grin of Tamir Rice, who reminded me so much of my own son. A book that made me proud when the outspokenness of Sandra Bland made me think of both of my daughters.

In the stories of these people, I see the depth and breadth of Black America. I see our pain and our promise. I see our struggle and our victory. I see our humanity, and I can only hope that readers will see it as well. As much as this book made me mourn the loss of those who died senselessly, it made me marvel at the resilience of those who rose up against all odds.

I am proud that Hassan Bennett used solitary confinement as a springboard to freedom, relentlessly studying the law until he could walk into a courtroom, face off against seasoned lawyers, and ultimately win his freedom. I am inspired by the stories that Tracy Martin told me about his heroic son, Trayvon. I am humbled by the fire of Geneva Reed-Veal, who has made good on her promise to tell the story of her daughter Sandra Bland.

More than anything, though, I'm compelled to keep moving forward, because for me, reliving the loss of Breonna Taylor and Alton Sterling and Michael Brown is not about heartbreak. It's about rejuvenation. It's about purpose. It's about movement.

As happy as I was to celebrate Derek Chauvin being convicted of murder in the death of George Floyd, I know that decision is an anomaly. I know because prosecutors like Timothy McGinty and Robert McCulloch and Daniel Cameron showed up again and again in the pages of this book, hiding behind the systems that allow them to act as defense attorneys for the police officers who kill Black people with impunity. I know because when federal convictions require "willful" violation of people's rights, they are ultimately designed to fail. I know because our criminal justice system is designed to maintain white supremacy, and dismantling that kind of system requires more than just protest. It requires strategy.

The demands in this book are drawn from my desire to see my people fight and win the equality we deserve. They are drawn from experiences that are in turns heartbreaking and uplifting. They are designed to comfort the families that have lost loved ones to America's racist systems.

We need mental health treatment so that people like Deborah Danner and Kawaski Trawick and Eleanor Bumpurs can live—through their illnesses. We need legislation so that violent or incompetent or racist police officers can be held accountable. We need the gumption to demand equal treatment in a country we built with our bare hands.

America is our country. Its wealth is built on our backs. Its capitalism depends on our consumption, and its future will be defined by our success. We demand much more than I could list in these pages, but these ten things are a damn good start.

ACKNOWLEDGMENTS

First, I want to thank my Lord and Savior Jesus Christ for the gift of writing. He used that gift to free me from the bondage of addiction, to snatch me from streets that consumed me, and to empower me to do more than I ever thought was possible. I'm grateful. Thanks to my agent, Jill Marr, who convinced me to write a book on race at a time when it was desperately needed. To my editor, Helene Atwan, thank you for providing the honest and insightful critique that made this work stronger. Thanks to the members of the Rally for Justice Coalition who made it possible for us to stand up together and demand the firing of police officers whose racist and offensive Facebook posts made them unworthy to serve our community. To WURD Radio, Radio One Philadelphia, the *Philadelphia Inquirer*, and WHYY, thank you for being the megaphone through which I speak. To my readers and listeners, thank you for your daily inspiration, for stopping me on the street to encourage me, for praying for me even when I don't know it. To the men and women of ManUpPHL, thank you for working so hard to help the young Black and Brown men whose lives are in danger not only from the gun violence in our streets but also from the systems that continually target them. To my family at Great Commission Church, thank you for your prayers. To my wife and children, my parents, my aunt, and all my extended family, thank you for loving me. Your love has taught me to love others, to seek justice, and to give of myself whenever possible. And finally, to the families of those featured in these pages, I acknowledge your hurt and promise to support your efforts both physically and financially as you continue to fight for the justice you so richly deserve.

NOTES

PREFACE

1. Chris Barber, "Public Enemy Number One: A Pragmatic Approach to America's Drug Problem," Richard Nixon Foundation, June 29, 2016, https://www.nixonfoundation.org/2016/06/26404.
2. Ronald Reagan, "Radio Address to the Nation on Federal Drug Policy," October 2, 1982, Ronald Reagan Presidential Library, https://www.reaganlibrary.gov/archives/speech/radio-address-nation-federal-drug-policy.
3. Matthew R. Pembleton, "George H. W. Bush's Biggest Failure? The War on Drugs," *Washington Post*, December 6, 2018, https://www.washingtonpost.com/outlook/2018/12/06/george-hw-bushs-biggest-failure-war-drugs.
4. Andrew Kaczynski, "Biden in 1993 Speech Pushing Crime Bill Warned of 'Predators on Our Streets' Who Were 'Beyond the Pale,'" CNN.com, March 7, 2019, https://www.cnn.com/2019/03/07/politics/biden-1993-speech-predators/index.html.
5. Ta-Nehisi Coates, "The Case for Reparations," *Atlantic*, June 2014, https://www.theatlantic.com/magazine/archive/2014/06/the-case-for-reparations/361631.
6. Roland G. Fryer Jr. et al., *Measuring Crack Cocaine and Its Impact* (Cambridge, MA: Harvard University Society of Fellows and NBER, April 2006), https://scholar.harvard.edu/files/fryer/files/fhlm_crack_cocaine_0.pdf.

CHAPTER 1: GEORGE FLOYD

1. Deborah J. Vagins and Jesselyn McCurdy, *Cracks in the System: Twenty Years of the Unjust Federal Crack Cocaine Law* (New York: American Civil Liberties Union, October 2006), https://www.aclu.org/other/cracks-system-20-years-unjust-federal-crack-cocaine-law.
2. CNN Wire Staff, "Obama Signs Bill Reducing Cocaine Sentencing Gap," August 3, 2010, https://www.cnn.com/2010/POLITICS/08/03/fair.sentencing/index.html.
3. Ezekiel Edwards et al., *A Tale of Two Countries: Racially Targeted Arrests in the Era of Marijuana Reform* (New York: American Civil Liberties Union, 2020), https://www.aclu.org/report/tale-two-countries-racially-targeted-arrests-era-marijuana-reform.
4. Associated Press, "George Floyd Transcript: Read It in Full Here," TwinCities.com, *Pioneer Press*, July 9, 2020, https://www.twincities.com/2020/07/09/george-floyd-transcript-read-it-in-full-here.
5. Bill Chappell and Vanessa Romo, "Chauvin Trial: Expert Says George Floyd Died Lack Oxygen, Not Fentanyl," NPR, updated April 8, 2021, https://www.npr.org/sections/trial-over-killing-of-george-floyd/2021/04/08/985347984/chauvin-trial-medical-expert-says-george-floyd-died-from-a-lack-of-oxygen.
6. Kaiser Family Foundation, "State Health Facts: Opioid Overdose Deaths by Race/Ethnicity," 2016, https://bit.ly/31IYoRr.
7. Institute for Justice, "Philadelphia Civil Forfeiture Machine Facts and Figures," last modified January 1, 2020, https://ij.org/philadelphia-facts-and-figures.
8. Wendy Sawyer and Peter Wagner, *Mass Incarceration: The Whole Pie 2020*

(Northampton, MA: Prison Policy Initiative, March 24, 2020), https://www.prisonpolicy.org/reports/pie2020.html.

9. Elle Lett et al., "Racial Inequity in Fatal US Police Shootings, 2015–2020," *Journal of Epidemiology and Community Health* 75, no. 4 (October 27, 2020), doi: 10.1136/jech-2020-215097.
10. Barbara Ferrer and John M. Connolly, "Racial Inequities in Drug Arrests: Treatment in Lieu of and After Incarceration," *American Journal of Public Health* 108, no. 8 (2018): 968–69, doi:10.2105/AJPH.2018.304575.
11. Pew Charitable Trusts, *More Imprisonment Does Not Reduce State Drug Problems* (March 2018), https://www.pewtrusts.org/-/media/assets/2018/03/pspp_more_imprisonment_does_not_reduce_state_drug_problems.pdf.
12. ACLU, "Asset Forfeiture Abuse," https://www.aclu.org/issues/criminal-law-reform/reforming-police/asset-forfeiture-abuse, accessed April 6, 2021.
13. Nielsen, "It's in the Bag: Black Consumers' Path to Purchase," Diverse Intelligence Series: 2019, https://www.nielsen.com/wp-content/uploads/sites/3/2019/09/2019-african-american-DIS-report.pdf.

CHAPTER 2: MICHAEL BROWN

1. Jesse Bogan and Walker Moskop, "What's Going to Happen to Canfield Green Apartments?," *St. Louis Post-Dispatch*, March 16, 2015, https://www.stltoday.com/news/local/metro/whats-going-to-happen-to-canfield-green-apartments/article_a358dfaf-2e7f-51b1-941b-69d542c0f5a0.html.
2. Denver Nicks, "How Ferguson Went from Middle Class to Poor in a Generation," *Time*, August 18, 2014, https://time.com/3138176/ferguson-demographic-change.
3. Josh Sanburn, "All the Ways Darren Wilson Described Being Afraid of Michael Brown," *Time*, November 25, 2014, https://time.com/3605346/darren-wilson-michael-brown-demon.
4. Larry Buchanan et al., "What Happened in Ferguson?," *New York Times*, August 10, 2015, https://www.nytimes.com/interactive/2014/08/13/us/ferguson-missouri-town-under-siege-after-police-shooting.html.
5. David Hunn and Kim Bell, "Why Was Michael Brown's Body Left There for Hours?," *St. Louis Post-Dispatch*, September 4, 2014, https://www.stltoday.com/news/local/crime-and-courts/why-was-michael-browns-body-left-there-for-hours/article_0b73ec58-c6a1-516e-882f-74d18a4246e0.html.
6. David G. Embrick, "Two Nations, Revisited: The Lynching of Black and Brown Bodies, Police Brutality, and Racial Control in 'Post-Racial' Amerikkka," *Critical Sociology* 41, no. 6 (2015): 835–43, https://doi.org/10.1177%2F0896920515591950.
7. "Understanding the Grand Jury Ruling on Michael Brown's Death," *PBS NewsHour*, November 24, 2014, https://www.pbs.org/newshour/show/understanding-grand-jury-ruling-michael-browns-death.
8. John Eligon, "Michael Brown Spent Last Weeks Grappling with Problems and Promise," *New York Times*, August 24, 2014, https://www.nytimes.com/2014/08/25/us/michael-brown-spent-last-weeks-grappling-with-lifes-mysteries.html.
9. Selwyn Duke, "Ferguson's Michael Brown: The Tall Tale of the 'Gentle Giant,'" *New American*, August 19, 2014, https://thenewamerican.com/ferguson-s-michael-brown-the-tall-tale-of-the-gentle-giant.
10. Calvin John Smiley and David Fakunle, "From 'Brute' to 'Thug': The Demonization and Criminalization of Unarmed Black Male Victims in America," *Journal of Human Behavior in the Social Environment* 26, no. 3–4 (2016): 350–66, https://www.ncbi.nlm.nih.gov/pmc/articles/PMC5004736.
11. Ben Grunwald and John Rappaport, "The Wandering Officer," *Yale Law Journal* 129, no. 6 (April 2020), https://www.yalelawjournal.org/article/the-wandering-officer.
12. Jeremy Kohler, "Statement of St. Louis Prosecuting Attorney Robert P. McCulloch,"

St. Louis Post-Dispatch, November 24, 2014, https://www.stltoday.com/news/local/crime-and-courts/statement-of-st-louis-prosecuting-attorney-robert-p-mcculloch/article_2becfef3-9b4b-5e1e-9043-f586f389ef91.html.

13. Erik Wemple, "Ferguson: How Can You Blame McCulloch for Blaming the Media?," *Washington Post*, November 25, 2014, https://www.washingtonpost.com/blogs/erik-wemple/wp/2014/11/25/ferguson-how-can-you-blame-mcculloch-for-blaming-the-media/.
14. Matt Ferner, "How Activists Ousted St. Louis County's Notorious Top Prosecutor Bob McCulloch," HuffPost, updated August 13, 2018, https://www.huffpost.com/entry/st-louis-county-missouri-prosecutor-bob-mcculloch-defeat_n_5b6e0c96e4b0530743c9f032.
15. Civil Rights Division, US Department of Justice (hereafter DOJ), *Department of Justice Report Regarding the Criminal Investigation into the Shooting Death of Michael Brown by Ferguson, Missouri Police Officer Darren Wilson* (Washington, DC: March 4, 2015), https://www.justice.gov/sites/default/files/opa/press-releases/attachments/2015/03/04/doj_report_on_shooting_of_michael_brown_1.pdf.
16. Civil Rights Division, DOJ, *Investigation of the Ferguson Police Department* (Washington, DC: March 4, 2015), https://www.justice.gov/sites/default/files/opa/press-releases/attachments/2015/03/04/ferguson_police_department_report_1.pdf.
17. Civil Rights Division, DOJ, *The Civil Rights Division's Pattern and Practice Police Reform Work: 1994–Present* (Washington, DC: January 2017), https://www.justice.gov/crt/file/922421/download.
18. "What Are Consent Decrees?" Criminal Justice Programs, https://www.criminaljusticeprograms.com/articles/what-are-consent-decrees, accessed March 29, 2021.
19. Civil Rights Division, DOJ, *Investigation of the Ferguson Police Department* (Washington, DC: March 4, 2015), https://www.justice.gov/sites/default/files/opa/press-releases/attachments/2015/03/04/ferguson_police_department_report_1.pdf.
20. Sharon Brett phone interview with author, February 15, 2021.
21. "Official Website of the Independent Monitor for the City of Ferguson, Missouri," Ferguson Monitor, https://fergusonmonitor.com, accessed March 29, 2021.
22. *US v. Ferguson, Missouri*, "Status Conference via Videoconference Before the Honorable Catherine D. Perry, United States District Judge," January 12, 2021, https://fergusonmonitor.com/wp-content/uploads/2021/02/January-12-2021-Transcript.pdf.

CHAPTER 3: HASSAN BENNETT

1. Solomon Jones, "Hassan Bennett on Classix 107.9 FM," Soundcloud.com, https://soundcloud.com/solomon-jones-10/hassan-bennett-your-voice-1079-fm, accessed March 29, 2021.
2. US Census Bureau, "QuickFacts," https://www.census.gov/quickfacts/fact/table/US/RHI225219, accessed March 29, 2021; Niraj Chokshi, "Black People More Likely to Be Wrongfully Convicted of Murder, Study Shows," *New York Times*, March 7, 2017, https://www.nytimes.com/2017/03/07/us/wrongful-convictions-race-exoneration.html.
3. Anthony Graves, *Infinite Hope: How Wrongful Conviction, Solitary Confinement, and 12 Years on Death Row Failed to Kill My Soul* (Boston: Beacon Press, 2018), 88.
4. Anthony Ray Hinton with Lara Love Hardin, *The Sun Does Shine: How I Found Life and Freedom on Death Row* (New York: St. Martin's Press, 2018), 155.
5. NAACP, "NAACP Death Penalty Fact Sheet: The Death Penalty Is Plagued with Racial Disparities," NAACP.org, January 17, 2017, https://www.naacp.org/latest/naacp-death-penalty-fact-sheet.
6. Scott Phillips and Justin F. Marceau, "Whom the State Kills," *Harvard Civil Rights–Civil Liberties Law Review*, University of Denver Legal Studies Research Paper No. 19-16, last updated July 30, 2020, http://dx.doi.org/10.2139/ssrn.3440828.

7. Innocence Project, "It's Time for All 50 States to Compensate the Wrongfully Convicted," Innocence Project, https://innocenceproject.org/compensation-all-50-states, accessed March 29, 2021.

CHAPTER 4: BREONNA TAYLOR

1. Allie Yang et al., "New Details Emerge in Chaotic Moments After Breonna Taylor Shooting," ABC News, November 18, 2020, https://abcnews.go.com/US/details-emerge-chaotic-moments-breonna-taylor-shooting/story?id=74254765.
2. Darcy Costello and Tessa Duvall, "911 Call from Breonna Taylor Shooting: 'Somebody Kicked in the Door and Shot My Girlfriend,'" *Louisville Courier Journal*, updated January 22, 2021, https://www.courier-journal.com/story/news/local/2020/05/28/breonna-taylor-shooting-911-call-details-aftermath-police-raid/5277489002.
3. WLKY News Louisville, "911 Call from Kenneth Walker," May 28, 2020, https://www.youtube.com/watch?v=GoEnRabtRhg.
4. Yang et al., "New Details Emerge in Chaotic Moments After Breonna Taylor Shooting."
5. Molly Olmstead, "What to Make of the New Developments in the Breonna Taylor Case," Slate.com, September 28, 2020, https://slate.com/news-and-politics/2020/09/breonna-taylor-case-new-evidence-investigation.html.
6. Alex Perez, "New Body Camera Footage Released in Breonna Taylor's Shooting," ABC News, October 9, 2020, https://www.youtube.com/watch?v=pdnrUSwbFn8.
7. Yang et al., "New Details Emerge in Chaotic Moments After Breonna Taylor Shooting."
8. Darcy Costello and Tessa Duvall, "Breonna Taylor Was Briefly Alive After Police Shot Her. But No One Tried to Treat Her," *Louisville Courier Journal*, updated March 13, 2021, https://www.courier-journal.com/story/news/crime/2020/07/17/breonna-taylor-lay-untouched-20-minutes-after-being-shot-records/5389881002.
9. Yang et al., "New Details Emerge in Chaotic Moments After Breonna Taylor Shooting."
10. President's Task Force on 21st Century Policing, *Final Report of the President's Task Force on 21st Century Policing* (Washington, DC: Office of Community Oriented Policing Services, May 2015), https://www.ojp.gov/library/abstracts/final-report-presidents-task-force-21st-century-policing.
11. Barak Ariel, William A. Farrar, and Alex Sutherland, "The Effect of Police Body-Worn Cameras on Use of Force and Citizens Complaints Against the Police: A Randomized Controlled Trial," *Journal of Quantitative Criminology* 31 (November 19, 2015): 509–35, https://doi.org/10.1007/s10940-014-9236-3.
12. David Yokum et al., "Randomized Controlled Trial of the Metropolitan Police Department Body-Worn Camera Program," The Lab @ DC and Metropolitan Police Department, https://bwc.thelab.dc.gov, accessed March 29, 2021.
13. Matthew Feeney, "'Hardcore' Body Camera Policies Could Do More Harm Than Good," Cato Institute, August 22, 2016, https://www.cato.org/commentary/hardcore-body-camera-policies-could-do-more-harm-good; Matthew Feeney, "Body Cameras Worth Deploying Despite Limited Impact," Cato Institute, November 1, 2017, https://www.cato.org/blog/body-cameras-worth-deploying-despite-limited-impact; Matthew Feeney, "Body Camera Studies Aren't Conclusive—Mandate Them Anyway," Cato Institute, September 28, 2015, https://www.cato.org/commentary/body-camera-studies-arent-conclusive-mandate-them-anyway.
14. NBC News, "Obama Requests $263 Million for Police Body Cameras, Training," NBCNews.com, December 1, 2014, https://www.nbcnews.com/politics/first-read/obama-requests-263-million-police-body-cameras-training-n259161.
15. Kevin Johnson, "Police Killings Highest in Two Decades," *USA Today*, updated

November 11, 2014, https://www.usatoday.com/story/news/nation/2014/11/11/police-killings-hundreds/18818663.

16. Jon Swaine and Ciara McCarthy, "Young Black Men Again Faced Highest Rate of US Police Killings in 2016," *Guardian*, January 8, 2017, https://www.theguardian.com/us-news/2017/jan/08/the-counted-police-killings-2016-young-black-men.
17. *Washington Post*, "Fatal Force," updated March 11, 2021, https://www.washingtonpost.com/graphics/investigations/police-shootings-database/.
18. Jason Riley, Marcus Green, and Travis Ragsdale, "Louisville Postal Inspector: No Packages of Interest at Slain EMT Breonna Taylor's Home," WDRB.com, May 16, 2020, https://www.wdrb.com/in-depth/louisville-postal-inspector-no-packages-of-interest-at-slain-emt-breonna-taylor-s-home/article_f25bbc06–96e4-11ea-9371-97b341bd2866.html.
19. Christina Carrega and Sabina Ghebremedhin, "Timeline: Inside the Investigation of Breonna Taylor's Killing and Its Aftermath," ABCNews.com, November 17, 2020, https://abcnews.go.com/US/timeline-inside-investigation-breonna-taylors-killing-aftermath/story?id=71217247.
20. Breonna's Law, "Ordinance No. 069, Series 2020," Louisville City Government, https://louisvilleky.gov/metro-council/document/breonna-taylor-law, accessed March 29, 2021.
21. *Guardian* Staff and Agencies, "Breonna Taylor: Grand Juror Speaks Out, Saying Homicide Charges Weren't Offered," October 20, 2020, https://www.theguardian.com/us-news/2020/oct/20/breonna-taylor-grand-juror-homicide-charges.
22. Emily Shapiro, "AG Cameron Defends Decision to Not Advise Breonna Taylor Grand Jury of More Charges," ABCNews.com, October 31, 2020, https://abcnews.go.com/US/ag-cameron-defends-decision-advise-breonna-taylor-grand/story?id=73940937.
23. Michelle Lou and Brandon Griggs, "A Proposed Tennessee Law Would Make It a Felony for Police Officers to Disable Their Body Cams," CNN.com, February 27, 2019, https://www.cnn.com/2019/02/27/us/tennessee-body-cam-felony-trnd.

CHAPTER 5: ERIC GARNER

1. Al Baker, J. David Goodman, and Benjamin Mueller, "Beyond the Chokehold: The Path to Eric Garner's Death," *New York Times*, June 13, 2015, https://www.nytimes.com/2015/06/14/nyregion/eric-garner-police-chokehold-staten-island.html.
2. "In the Matter of Charges and Specifications Against Police Officer Daniel Pantaleo," New York Police Department, Case No. 2018-19274, https://int.nyt.com/data/documenthelper/1645-read-the-judges-opinion/1ab51bece4671aa10d11/optimized/full.pdf, accessed March 29, 2021.
3. Ken Murray et al., "Staten Island Man Dies After NYPD Cop Puts Him in Chokehold—See the Video," *New York Daily News*, December 3, 2014, https://www.nydailynews.com/new-york/staten-island-man-dies-puts-choke-hold-article-1.1871486.
4. "In the Matter of Charges and Specifications Against Police Officer Daniel Pantaleo," New York Police Department.
5. Baker, Goodman, and Mueller, "Beyond the Chokehold."
6. Wesley Lowery, " 'I Can't Breathe': Five Years After Eric Garner Died in Struggle with New York Police, Resolution Still Elusive," *Washington Post*, June 13, 2019, https://www.washingtonpost.com/national/i-cant-breathe-five-years-after-eric-garner-died-in-struggle-with-new-york-police-resolution-still-elusive/2019/06/13/23d7fad8-78f5-11e9-bd25-c989555e7766_story.html.
7. Harry Siegel, "The Lonesome Death of Eric Garner," *New York Daily News*, December 13, 2014, https://www.nydailynews.com/opinion/harry-siegel-lonesome-death-eric-garner-article-1.2032281.
8. Lowery, "I Can't Breathe."

9. Associated Press, "Hospital to Pay $1M to Family of Eric Garner," CBS12.com, February 23, 2016, https://cbs12.com/news/nation-world/hospital-to-pay-1m-to-family-of-eric-garner.
10. Baker, Goodman, and Mueller, "Beyond the Chokehold."
11. Lowery, "I Can't Breathe."
12. New York State Assembly, Bill No. A09332, "An Act to Repeal Section 50-A of the Civil Rights Law, Related to Personnel Records of Police Officers, Firefighters and Corrections Officers," New York State Assembly, https://nyassembly.gov/leg/?default_fld=&bn=9332&term=2015&Summary=Y&Memo=Y, accessed March 29, 2021.
13. J. David Goodman and Joseph Goldstein, "Handling of New York Chokehold Cases 'Disappointing,' Review Board Chief Says," *New York Times*, August 5, 2014, https://www.nytimes.com/2014/08/06/nyregion/handling-of-new-york-chokehold-cases-disappointing-review-board-chief-says.html.
14. Tom Wrobleski, "Law Enforcement Unions Endorse Staten Island District Attorney Daniel Donovan for Third Term," SILive.com, updated January 3, 2019, https://www.silive.com/news/2011/09/law_enforcement_unions_donovan.html.
15. James Queally and Lauren Raab, "Dan Donovan, Prosecutor in Eric Garner Death Case, Wins House Seat," *Los Angeles Times*, May 5, 2015, https://www.latimes.com/nation/politics/politicsnow/la-pn-dan-donovan-congress-20150505-story.html.
16. Lowery, "I Can't Breathe."
17. Lowery, "I Can't Breathe."
18. Michael Wilson, "How the NYPD Commissioner Grappled with the Eric Garner Decision," *New York Times*, August 19, 2019, https://www.nytimes.com/2019/08/19/nyregion/nypd-police-commissioner-pantaleo.html.
19. Missouri Court of Appeals Western District, "Kevin Schnell, Appellant v. Karl Zobrist, et al., Respondents," June 29, 2010, https://www.courts.mo.gov/file.jsp?id=39783.
20. "Regional Briefs: Miscarriage Suit Settled," *Oklahoman*, October 19, 2008, https://oklahoman.com/article/3312976/regional-briefs-miscarriage-suit-settled.
21. Sonia Moghe, "Disciplinary Record of Ex-Officer Who Held Eric Garner in Chokehold Is Finally Released," CNN.com, updated June 23, 2020, https://www.cnn.com/2020/06/23/us/eric-garner-officer-misconduct-complaints/index.html.

CHAPTER 6: ALTON STERLING

1. Gabe Gutierrez and Corky Siemaszko, "'Full of Joy': Family Mourns Alton Sterling, Louisiana Man Killed by Cops," NBCNews.com, July 6, 2016, https://www.nbcnews.com/news/us-news/alton-sterling-louisiana-man-killed-cops-mourned-family-n604781.
2. Diana Samuels, "'He's Got a Pistol in His Pocket': Baton Rouge Police Release Alton Sterling 911 Calls," *Times-Picayune*, updated July 12, 2019, https://www.nola.com/news/crime_police/article_7aa17d7f-04c6-5d6b-aa31-ddddca413949.html.
3. Jim Mustian and Lea Skene, "New Alton Sterling Shooting Videos Show Deadly, Heated Scene at Triple S," *Advocate*, March 30, 2018, https://www.theadvocate.com/baton_rouge/news/alton_sterling/article_209c1f62-33c7-11e8-a2c8-179ff7c92a3f.html.
4. CGTN, "Alton Sterling Shooting: Bodycam Footage Released by Baton Rouge Police," China Global TV Network, https://www.youtube.com/watch?v=jgX7Az8eJCw.
5. Matthew Teague and Oliver Laughland, "Alton Sterling Shooting: New Footage Appears to Show Police Taking Gun from Body," *Guardian*, July 7, 2016, https://www.theguardian.com/us-news/2016/jul/06/alton-sterling-gun-baton-rouge-new-video.
6. US Census Bureau, "Baton Rouge City, Louisiana Profile," Data.Census.gov, https://data.census.gov/cedsci/all?q=baton%20rouge%20population%202016, accessed March 30, 2021.

7. Mark Berman, "Baton Rouge Prosecutor Says He Will Recuse Himself from Investigation into Alton Sterling's Death," *Washington Post*, July 11, 2016, https://www.washingtonpost.com/news/post-nation/wp/2016/07/11/prosecutor-says-he-will-recuse-himself-from-investigation-into-alton-sterlings-death.
8. Rebecca Santana, "Chief Apologizes over Hiring of Officer Who Shot Black Man," Associated Press, August 1, 2019, https://apnews.com/article/f6f14016c7b64a6d883a35a48b330298.
9. Rebecca Brown, "It's Time to Make Police Disciplinary Records Public," Innocence Project, July 2, 2020, https://innocenceproject.org/its-time-to-make-police-disciplinary-records-public.
10. Tricia Bishop, "The Lesson in Alton Sterling's Criminal Past," *Baltimore Sun*, July 7, 2016, https://www.baltimoresun.com/opinion/op-ed/bs-ed-bishop-0708-20160707-story.html.
11. Phillip M. Bailey and Darcy Costello, "Breonna Taylor's Ex-Boyfriend: Plea Deal Tried to Get Me to Falsely Incriminate Her," *Louisville Courier Journal*, September 1, 2020, https://www.courier-journal.com/story/news/local/breonna-taylor/2020/09/01/breonna-taylors-ex-says-prosecutor-trying-cover-up-fatal-shooting/3453352001/.
12. Gutierrez and Siemaszko, " 'Full of Joy.' "
13. Richard A. Webster, "Baton Rouge DA Won't Prosecute 100 of 185 Arrested in Alton Sterling Protests," *Times-Picayune*, updated July 19, 2019, https://www.nola.com/news/crime_police/article_6a56cfe1-2618-534c-a542-4e97ff743c8d.html.
14. Anna Merod, "BLM Activist DeRay McKesson [sic] Sues City of Baton Rouge for Mass Arrests," NBCNews.com, August 4, 2016, https://www.nbcnews.com/news/us-news/blm-activist-deray-mckesson-sues-city-baton-rouge-mass-arrests-n623286.
15. Civil Rights Division, DOJ, "Title 18 U.S. Code Section 242, Deprivation of Rights Under Color of Law," updated May 19, 2020, https://www.justice.gov/crt/deprivation-rights-under-color-law.
16. *Advocate* Staff Report, "Alton Sterling Decision: Read AG's Full Statement, Report on Choice Not to Charge Officers," March 27, 2018, https://www.theadvocate.com/baton_rouge/news/alton_sterling/article_9dc82e16-31d5-11e8-a376-afe0629dbaaa.html.
17. Colleen Kane Gielskie, "Not Charging the Officers Who Killed Alton Sterling Is a Travesty," American Civil Liberties Union of Louisiana, March 30, 2018, https://www.aclu.org/blog/criminal-law-reform/reforming-police/not-charging-officers-who-killed-alton-sterling-travesty.
18. Emily Shapiro, "Why the Justice Department Didn't Press Charges in the Alton Sterling Case," ABCNews.com, May 3, 2017, https://abcnews.go.com/US/justice-department-decided-press-charges-officers-alton-sterling/story?id=47176525.
19. Courtney Connley, "DOJ Not Expected to File Charges in Alton Sterling Case," ABCNews.com, May 2, 2017, https://abcnews.go.com/US/doj-expected-file-charges-alton-sterling-case/story?id=47167932.
20. Shapiro, "Why the Justice Department Didn't Press Charges in the Alton Sterling Case."
21. Brian Bowling and Andrew Conte, "Trib Investigation: Cops Often Let Off Hook for Civil Rights Complaints," *Tribune-Review* (Pittsburgh), March 12, 2016, https://archive.triblive.com/news/nation/trib-investigation-cops-often-let-off-hook-for-civil-rights-complaints.

CHAPTER 7: TAMIR RICE

1. CNN, "911 Caller: Gun Might Be Fake," CNN YouTube channel, November 26, 2014, https://www.youtube.com/watch?v=Xjf89P6kaEc.
2. *USA Today*, "Full Tamir Rice Autopsy Report," Scribd.com, https://www.scribd.com/doc/249972489/Full-Tamir-Rice-autospy-report, accessed March 30, 2021.

3. Kristina Bravo, "Cleveland Police Officer Fatally Shoots 12-Year-Old Boy Carrying a Toy Firearm," TakePart, November 23, 2014, http://www.takepart.com/article/2014/11/23/cleveland-police-officer-fatally-shoots-12-year-old-boy-carrying-toy-firearm/.
4. Al Sharpton, "Why Did Cleveland Police Shoot a 12-Year-Old?," *Politics Nation*, MSNBC, December 2, 2014, https://www.msnbc.com/politicsnation/watch/why-did-cleveland-police-shoot-a-12-year-old-366337091561.
5. Sharpton, "Why Did Cleveland Police Shoot a 12-Year-Old?"
6. Jamiel Lynch, Christina Carrega, and Steve Almasy, "Justice Department Won't Pursue Charges Against Officers in Tamir Rice Shooting," CNN.com, December 29, 2020, https://www.cnn.com/2020/12/29/us/tamir-rice-shooting-no-federal-charges/index.html.
7. Eric Levenson, Evan Simko-Bednarski, and Joel Williams, "Officer in Tamir Rice Shooting: 'We Were Basically Sitting Ducks,'" CNN.com, April 25, 2017, https://www.cnn.com/2017/04/25/us/tamir-rice-police-interview.
8. WKYC.com, "Timothy Loehmann Personnel File Independence Police Department," Scribd.com, September 5, 2013, https://www.scribd.com/document/249093481/Loehmann-Personnel-File.
9. Associated Press, "Six Cleveland Officers Sacked After 137 Shots Killed Two Unarmed Black People," *Guardian*, January 26, 2016, https://www.theguardian.com/us-news/2016/jan/27/cleveland-fatal-shooting-timothy-russell-malissa-williams-officers-fired.
10. Shaila Dewan and Richard A. Oppel Jr., "In Tamir Rice Case, Many Errors by Cleveland Police, Then a Fatal One," *New York Times*, January 22, 2015, https://www.nytimes.com/2015/01/23/us/in-tamir-rice-shooting-in-cleveland-many-errors-by-police-then-a-fatal-one.html.
11. *New York Times*, "Judge Ronald B. Adrine's Ruling on the Cleveland Officers Involved in the Tamir Rice Shooting," June 11, 2015, https://www.nytimes.com/interactive/2015/06/11/us/document-cleveland-judge-to-charge-officers-in-tamir-rice-death.html.
12. Cleveland Municipal Court, Affidavits Relating to Timothy Loehmann and Frank Garmback, filed June 11, 2015, https://assets.documentcloud.org/documents/2096885/cleveland-judge-to-charge-officers-in-tamir-rice.pdf.
13. Richard Perex-Pena and Mitch Smith, "Cleveland Judge Finds Probable Cause to Arrest Officers in Tamir Rice Death," *New York Times*, June 11, 2015, https://www.nytimes.com/2015/06/12/us/judge-finds-probable-cause-to-charge-officers-in-tamir-rice-death.html.
14. Emily Shapiro, "Tamir Rice Case: Prosecutor Abused, Manipulated Grand Jury Process, Family Attorneys Say," ABC News, December 28, 2015, https://abcnews.go.com/US/tamir-rice-case-prosecutor-abused-manipulated-grand-jury/story?id=35979452.
15. Richard A. Oppel and Mitch Smith, "Tamir Rice's Family Clashes with Prosecutor over Police Shooting," *New York Times*, December 23, 2015, https://www.nytimes.com/2015/12/24/us/tamir-rices-family-and-prosecutor-quarrel-over-release-of-evidence.html.
16. Leah Donnella, "Must-Read Reactions to Grand Jury Decision in Tamir Rice Case," *CodeSwitch*, NPR, December 28, 2015, https://www.npr.org/sections/codeswitch/2015/12/28/460590173/no-charges-for-cop-who-killed-tamir-rice-some-must-read-reactions.
17. Jaeah Lee, "Two Expert Reports Slam Cleveland Cops for 'Reckless' Killing of Tamir Rice," *Mother Jones*, December 1, 2015, https://www.motherjones.com/politics/2015/12/two-experts-police-shooting-tamir-rice-reckless-avoidable/.
18. Sean Flynn, "The Tamir Rice Story: How to Make a Police Shooting Disappear," *GQ*, July 14, 2016, https://www.gq.com/story/tamir-rice-story.

19. Phillip Atiba Goff et al., "The Essence of Innocence: Consequences of Dehumanizing Black Children," *Journal of Personality and Social Psychology* 106, no. 4 (February 2014), https://www.apa.org/pubs/journals/releases/psp-a0035663.pdf.
20. American Psychological Association, "Black Boys Viewed as Older, Less Innocent Than Whites, Research Finds," press release, APA.org, 2014, https://www.apa.org/news/press/releases/2014/03/black-boys-older.
21. Associated Press, "Grand Jury Declines to Indict Cleveland Officer in Fatal Shooting of 12-Year-Old Tamir Rice," *Los Angeles Times*, December 28, 2015, https://www.latimes.com/nation/la-na-tamir-rice-grand-jury-20151228-story.html.
22. Timothy Williams and Mitch Smith, "Cleveland Officer Will Not Face Charges in Tamir Rice Shooting Death," *New York Times*, December 28, 2015, https://www.nytimes.com/2015/12/29/us/tamir-rice-police-shootiing-cleveland.html.
23. Laura Wagner and Merrit Kennedy, "Grand Jury Declines to Indict Police Officers in Tamir Rice Investigation," *The Two-Way*, NPR, December 28, 2015, https://www.npr.org/sections/thetwo-way/2015/12/28/461293703/grand-jury-declines-to-indict-police-officers-in-tamir-rice-investigation.
24. Adam Ferrise, "Cleveland Officer Frank Garmback's Suspension Halved for Role in Tamir Rice Shooting," Cleveland.com, updated January 30, 2019, https://www.cleveland.com/metro/2018/07/cleveland_officer_frank_garmba.html.
25. Human Rights Watch, *Shielded from Justice: Police Brutality and Accountability in the United States*, HRW.org, https://www.hrw.org/legacy/reports98/police/uspo31.htm, accessed March 30, 2021.
26. Associated Press, "Tamir Rice's Family Asks Justice Department to Reopen Case into Police Killing," NBC News, April 16, 2021, https://www.nbcnews.com/news/us-news/tamir-rice-s-family-asks-justice-department-reopen-case-police-n1264279.

CHAPTER 8: TRAYVON MARTIN

1. NBA.com Staff, "2012 NBA All-Star Recap," NBA.com, August 24, 2017, https://www.nba.com/history/all-star/2012.
2. Sam Baldwin, "Transcript of George Zimmerman's Call to the Police," *Mother Jones*, https://www.documentcloud.org/documents/326700-full-transcript-zimmerman.html, accessed March 30, 2021.
3. CNN Wire Staff, "Timeline of Events in Trayvon Martin Case," CNN, April 23, 2012, https://www.cnn.com/2012/04/23/justice/florida-zimmerman-timeline/index.html.
4. CNN Newsroom, "Continuing Zimmerman Trial Coverage; Trayvon Martin's Girlfriend Testifies," CNN.com, June 26, 2013, http://edition.cnn.com/TRANSCRIPTS/1306/26/cnr.10.html.
5. Crimesider Staff, "911 Calls Released in Trayvon Martin Fatal Shooting," CBSNews.com, July 12, 2013, https://www.cbsnews.com/news/911-calls-released-in-trayvon-martin-fatal-shooting.
6. Greg Botelho, "What Happened the Night Trayvon Martin Died," CNN.com, May 23, 2012, https://www.cnn.com/2012/05/18/justice/florida-teen-shooting-details.
7. Solomon Jones, "Solomon Jones and Tracy Martin: Two Dads Talking About Trayvon," *Philadelphia Inquirer*, March 3, 2015, https://www.inquirer.com/philly/living/20150303_Solomon_Jones_and_Tracy_Martin__Two_dads_talking_about_Trayvon.html.
8. Edward B. Colby and Gilma Avalos, "Nothing to Dispute Sanford Shooter's Self-Defense Claim in Miami Boy's Death: Police Chief," NBCMiami.com, March 21, 2012, https://www.nbcmiami.com/news/local/nothing-to-dispute-sanford-shooters-self-defense-claim-in-miami-boys-death-police-chief/2036351.
9. National Conference of State Legislatures, "Self Defense and 'Stand Your Ground,'" NCSL.com, May 26, 2020, https://www.ncsl.org/research/civil-and-criminal-justice/self-defense-and-stand-your-ground.aspx.

10. Dennis Baxley, "Stand Your Ground," *Star-Banner* (Ocala, Florida), April 1, 2012, https://www.ocala.com/article/LK/20120401/Opinion/604140920/OS.
11. Rene Stutzman and *Orlando Sentinel*, "George Zimmerman's Father: My Son Is Not Racist, Did Not Confront Trayvon Martin," *Orlando Sentinel*, March 15, 2012, https://www.orlandosentinel.com/news/os-trayvon-martin-shooting-zimmerman-letter-20120315-story.html.
12. Alexis Garrett Stodghill, "George Zimmerman Not a Member of Recognized Neighborhood Watch Organization," The Grio, March 21, 2012, https://thegrio.com/2012/03/21/zimmerman-not-a-member-of-recognized-neighborhood-watch-organization.
13. Krissah Thompson and Scott Wilson, "Obama on Trayvon Martin: 'If I Had a Son He'd Look Like Trayvon,'" *Washington Post*, March 23, 2012, https://www.washingtonpost.com/politics/obama-if-i-had-a-son-hed-look-like-trayvon/2012/03/23/gIQApKPpVS_story.html.
14. Serge F. Kovaleski and Jennifer Preston, "'I Am Sorry,' Zimmerman Says, as Bail Set at $150,000," *New York Times*, April 20, 2012, https://www.nytimes.com/2012/04/21/us/george-zimmerman-bail-hearing.html.
15. Matt Gutman and Colleen Curry, "George Zimmerman Prepared to Flee U.S. with $130,000 Judge Says," ABCNews.com, July 5, 2012, https://abcnews.go.com/US/judge-george-zimmerman-prepared-flee-country/story?id=16715647.
16. CNN Wire Staff, "Zimmerman Asks for Another New Judge," CNN.com, July 14, 2012, https://edition.cnn.com/2012/07/13/justice/florida-teen-shooting/index.html.
17. Mark Memmott, "Read: Instructions for the Jury in Trial of George Zimmerman," *The Two-Way*, NPR, July 12, 2013, https://www.npr.org/sections/thetwo-way/2013/07/12/201410108/read-instructions-for-the-jury-in-trial-of-george-zimmerman.
18. Richard Luscombe, "Jury Hears Emotional Opening Statements in George Zimmerman Trial," *Guardian*, June 24, 2013, https://www.theguardian.com/world/2013/jun/24/george-zimmerman-trial-opening-statements.
19. *Orlando Sentinel*, "CNN Transcript: Juror B-37 Talks About the Zimmerman Verdict," July 15, 2013, https://www.orlandosentinel.com/news/os-xpm-2013-07-15-os-cnn-transcript-george-zimmerman-juror-speaks-20130715-story.html.
20. John Paul Wilson, Kurt Hugenberg, and Nicholas O. Rule, "Racial Bias in Judgments of Physical Size and Formidability: From Size to Threat," *Journal of Personality and Social Psychology* 113, no. 1 (March 2017): 59–80, https://doi.org/10.1037/pspi0000092.
21. Rukmani Bhatia, "Untangling the Gun Lobby's Web of Self-Defense and Human Rights: Peddling False Rights, Profiting Off Fear," Center for American Progress, August 12, 2020, https://www.americanprogress.org/issues/guns-crime/reports/2020/08/12/489284/untangling-gun-lobbys-web-self-defense-human-rights.
22. Bhatia, "Untangling the Gun Lobby's Web of Self-Defense and Human Rights."
23. Andrew R. Morral and Rosanna Smart, "'Stand Your Ground' Laws May Be Causing More Harm Than Good," *The Rand Blog*, September 12, 2019, https://www.rand.org/blog/2019/09/stand-your-ground-laws-increase-violence.html.
24. Richard Florida, "It's Not Just Zimmerman: Race Matters a Lot in 'Stand Your Ground' Verdicts," Bloomberg CityLab, July 15, 2013, https://www.bloomberg.com/news/articles/2013-07-15/it-s-not-just-zimmerman-race-matters-a-lot-in-stand-your-ground-verdicts.
25. Erik Ortiz, "'Stand Your Ground' in Florida Could Be Expanded Under DeSantis' 'Anti-Mob' Proposal," NBCNews.com, November 12, 2020, https://www.nbcnews.com/news/us-news/stand-your-ground-florida-could-be-expanded-under-desantis-anti-n1247555.

CHAPTER 9: DEBORAH DANNER

1. Chelsia Rose Marcius and Larry McShane, "Deborah Danner, Bronx Woman Killed by NYPD, Was 'Screaming and Yelling' to Be Left Alone Before Fatal Shooting," *New York Daily News*, February 1, 2018, https://www.nydailynews.com/new-york/bronx/deborah-danner-asked-left-fatal-nypd-shooting-article-1.3793532.
2. James C. McKinley Jr. and Joseph Goldstein, "Officer Testifies He Tried to Grab Woman Before Fatal Shooting," *New York Times*, February 13, 2018, https://www.nytimes.com/2018/02/13/nyregion/police-murder-trial-barry.html.
3. James C. McKinley Jr., "Was the Police Shooting of a Psychotic Woman Justified? D.A. Says No," *New York Times*, January 30, 2018, https://www.nytimes.com/2018/01/30/nyregion/fatal-police-shooting-trial.html.
4. McKinley and Goldstein, "Officer Testifies He Tried to Grab Woman Before Fatal Shooting."
5. Marcius and McShane, "Deborah Danner, Bronx Woman Killed by NYPD, Was 'Screaming and Yelling' to Be Left Alone Before Fatal Shooting."
6. McKinley and Goldstein, "Officer Testifies He Tried to Grab Woman Before Fatal Shooting."
7. Eli Rosenberg and Ashley Southall, "In Quick Response, de Blasio Calls Fatal Shooting of Mentally Ill Woman 'Unacceptable,'" *New York Times*, October 19, 2016, https://www.nytimes.com/2016/10/20/nyregion/nypd-sergeant-fatal-shooting-bronx-woman.html.
8. US Department of Health and Human Services Office of Minority Health, "Mental and Behavioral Health—African Americans," https://www.minorityhealth.hhs.gov/omh/browse.aspx?lvl=4&lvlid=24, accessed March 30, 2021.
9. Division of Diversity and Health Equity, Phillip Murray, MD, Danielle Hairston, MD, and the Council on Minority Mental Health and Health Disparities, "Guides and Toolkits: Mental Health Facts for African Americans," American Psychiatric Association, https://www.psychiatry.org/psychiatrists/cultural-competency/education/african-american-patients.
10. Eric Umansky, "It Wasn't the First Time the NYPD Killed Someone in Crisis. For Kawaski Trawick, It Only Took 112 Seconds," ProPublica, December 4, 2020, https://www.propublica.org/article/it-wasnt-the-first-time-the-nypd-killed-someone-in-crisis-for-kawaski-trawick-it-only-took-112-seconds.
11. Doris A. Fuller, H. Richard Lamb, MD, Michael Biasotti, and John Snook, *Overlooked in the Undercounted: The Role of Mental Illness in Fatal Law Enforcement Encounters* (Arlington, VA: Treatment Advocacy Center, December 2015), https://www.treatmentadvocacycenter.org/storage/documents/overlooked-in-the-undercounted.pdf.
12. Alexandria Sifferlin, "Untreated Mentally Ill 16 Times More Likely to Be Killed by Police, Study Says," Time.com, December 10, 2015, https://time.com/4144276/mentally-ill-police-killings-study.
13. *Washington Post*, "Fatal Force Database," updated March 11, 2021, https://www.washingtonpost.com/graphics/investigations/police-shootings-database/.
14. National Alliance on Mental Illness, "Jailing People with Mental Illness," Nami.org, https://www.nami.org/Advocacy/Policy-Priorities/Divert-from-Justice-Involvement/Jailing-People-with-Mental-Illness, accessed April 1, 2021.
15. William G. Brooks III, "Police Need More Mental Health Training," *The Hill*, February 22, 2018, https://thehill.com/opinion/healthcare/375040-police-need-more-mental-health-training.
16. Deborah Danner, "Living with Schizophrenia," DocumentCloud.org, January 28, 2012, https://assets.documentcloud.org/documents/3146953/Living-With-Schizophrenia-by-Deborah-Danner.pdf.

17. Alan Feuer, "Fatal Police Shooting in Bronx Echoes One from 32 Years Ago," *New York Times*, October 19, 2016, https://www.nytimes.com/2016/10/20/nyregion/fatal-police-shooting-in-bronx-echoes-one-from-32-years-ago.html.
18. Stuart Butler and Nehath Sheriff, *Innovative Solutions to Address the Mental Health Crisis: Shifting Away from Police as First Responders* (Washington, DC: Brookings Institution, November 23, 2020), https://www.brookings.edu/research/innovative-solutions-to-address-the-mental-health-crisis-shifting-away-from-police-as-first-responders.
19. Grace Hauck, "Police Have Shot People Experiencing a Mental Health Crisis. Who Should You Call Instead?," *USA Today*, September 18, 2020, https://www.usatoday.com/story/news/nation/2020/09/18/police-shooting-mental-health-solutions-training-defund/5763145002.
20. Butler and Sheriff, *Innovative Solutions to Address the Mental Health Crisis*.
21. US Census Bureau, "Quick Facts: Alexandria, Kentucky," Census.gov, https://www.census.gov/quickfacts/fact/table/alexandriacitykentucky/SEX255219, accessed April 1, 2020.
22. Josh Wood, "The US Police Department That Decided to Hire Social Workers," *Guardian*, September 19, 2020, https://www.theguardian.com/us-news/2020/sep/19/alexandria-kentucky-police-social-workers.
23. National Association of Social Workers (NASW), Connecticut Chapter, "Testimony on Utilization of Social Workers by Police Departments," NASWCT.org, October 1, 2020, http://naswct.org/testimony/testimony-on-utilization-of-social-workers-by-police-departments.
24. Ari Shapiro, "'CAHOOTS': How Social Workers and Police Share Responsibilities in Eugene, Oregon," *All Things Considered*, NPR, June 10, 2020, https://www.npr.org/2020/06/10/874339977/cahoots-how-social-workers-and-police-share-responsibilities-in-eugene-oregon.
25. Mike Desmond, "'I Don't Feel Comfortable Accompanying Police Anywhere,' Says Social Worker about New Plan," WBFO, NPR, September 18, 2020, https://news.wbfo.org/post/i-dont-feel-comfortable-accompanying-police-anywhere-says-social-worker-about-new-plan.
26. Zach Norris, *Defund Fear: Safety Without Policing, Prisons, and Punishment* (Boston: Beacon Press, 2020).

CHAPTER 10: SANDRA BLAND

1. WURD Radio, "Wake Up with WURD 4.21.16—Maria Hamilton and Geneva Reed-Veale [sic]," April 21, 2016, Soundcould.com, https://soundcloud.com/onwurd/wake-up-with-wurd-4-21-16-1.
2. Sandra Bland, "Sandy Speaks—Friday April 10, 2015 (Unite or Incite)," Sandy Speaks, YouTube, July 24, 2015, https://www.youtube.com/watch?v=YsTgyabGtL4.
3. WURD Radio, "Wake Up with WURD 4.21.16—Maria Hamilton and Geneva Reed-Veale [sic]."
4. Ryan Grim, "The Transcript of Sandra Bland's Arrest Is as Revealing as the Video," HuffPost.com, July 23, 2015, https://www.huffpost.com/entry/sandra-bland-arrest-transcript_n_55b03a88e4b0a9b94853b1f1.
5. David A. Graham, "A Perjury Charge for the Cop Who Pulled Over Sandra Bland," *Atlantic*, January 6, 2016, https://www.theatlantic.com/national/archive/2016/01/sandra-bland-trooper-indicted-for-perjury/422976.
6. E. Ann Carson and Mary P. Cowhig, "Mortality in Local Jails, 2000–2016—Statistical Tables," DOJ, Office of Justice Programs, Bureau of Justice Statistics, February 2020, https://www.bjs.gov/content/pub/pdf/mlj0016st.pdf.
7. Carson and Cowhig, "Mortality in Local Jails, 2000–2016—Statistical Tables."

8. Pierre Thomas, John Kelly, and Tonya Simpson, "ABC News Analysis of Police Arrests Nationwide Reveals Stark Racial Disparity," ABCNews.com, June 11, 2020, https://abcnews.go.com/US/abc-news-analysis-police-arrests-nationwide-reveals-stark/story?id=71188546.
9. Thomas, Kelly, and Simpson, "ABC News Analysis of Police Arrests Nationwide Reveals Stark Racial Disparity."
10. *New York Times*, "Sandra Bland's Jail-Booking Screening Form," July 23, 2015, https://www.nytimes.com/interactive/2015/07/23/us/document-sandra-bland-jail-booking-screening-form.html.
11. David Montgomery and Michael Wines, "Dispute over Sandra Bland's Mental State Follows Death in a Texas Jail," *New York Times*, July 22, 2015, https://www.nytimes.com/2015/07/23/us/sandra-blands-family-says-video-sheds-no-light-on-reason-for-her-arrest.html.
12. Texas Department of Public Safety, Texas Rangers, "Questionable Death, Waller County, Hempstead, Victim Bland, Sandra (B/F)," Clearinghouse.net, July 20, 2015, https://www.clearinghouse.net/chDocs/public/JC-TX-0025-0008.pdf.
13. Sarah Begley, "Sandra Bland's Friend Haunted by Missed Voicemail," *Time*, July 24, 2015, https://time.com/3970823/sandra-bland-voicemail.
14. Texas Department of Public Safety, Texas Rangers, "Questionable Death, Waller County, Hempstead, Victim Bland, Sandra (B/F)."
15. WURD Radio, "Wake Up with WURD 4.21.16—Maria Hamilton and Geneva Reed-Veale [sic]."
16. *Texas Tribune*, "Geneva Reed-Veal, Individually and as Mother and Personal Representative of the Estate of Sandra Bland, deceased, v. Brian Encinia, the Texas Department of Public Safety et al.," filed August 4, 2015, https://static.texastribune.org/media/documents/Bland_lawsuit.pdf.
17. Geoff Ziezulewicz and William Bird, "Woman from Chicago Area Found Dead in Texas Jail Cell," July 16, 2015, *Chicago Tribune*, https://www.chicagotribune.com/suburbs/naperville-sun/ct-nvs-sandra-bland-death-naperville-st-0717-20150715-story.html.
18. Graham, "A Perjury Charge for the Cop Who Pulled Over Sandra Bland."
19. Graham, "A Perjury Charge for the Cop Who Pulled Over Sandra Bland."
20. Jonathan Silver, "Sandra Bland's Family Settles Wrongful Death Lawsuit, Lawyer Says," TexasTribune.org, September 15, 2016, https://www.texastribune.org/2016/09/15/sandra-blands-family-settles-wrongful-death-lawsui.
21. David Harris, *Profiles in Injustice: Why Racial Profiling Cannot Work* (New York: New Press, 2003).
22. City of Houston, *Behavioral Health Advocacy, Sandra Bland Act*, Legislative Report 2017, http://www.houstontx.gov/txlege/sb-1849-sandra-bland-act, accessed March 30, 2021.
23. James Barragán, "Law Enforcement Groups Oppose Some of the Bills Filed in Response to Sandra Bland's Death," *Dallas Morning News*, March 20, 2017, https://www.dallasnews.com/news/politics/2017/03/20/law-enforcement-groups-oppose-some-of-the-bills-filed-in-response-to-sandra-bland-s-death.
24. Paul J. Weber, "Family Says Weakened Sandra Bland Act in Texas Is Gut-Wrenching," *Chicago Tribune*, March 14, 2017, https://www.chicagotribune.com/nation-world/ct-sandra-bland-act-texas-20170513-story.html.

SOLOMON JONES is an *Essence* best-selling author and an award-winning columnist for the *Philadelphia Inquirer*. He is a radio host for WURD Radio and Classix 107.9 in Philadelphia, as well as a blogger for WHYY. As a journalist and activist, he has been featured nationally on NPR's *Morning Edition*, WHYY, *Nightline*, CNN Headline News, and in *Essence* magazine. In 2019, Jones formed the Rally for Justice Coalition with a multitude of civil rights organizations. The coalition's efforts resulted in the firing of over a dozen Philadelphia police officers who espoused racist rhetoric online. Jones lives in Philadelphia with his wife and two youngest children, where he continues his advocacy and activism.